**Billy Graham
Evangelistic Association**

Dear Friend,

I am pleased to send you this copy of *How Sweet the Sound* by George Beverly Shea, who has been a good friend of my father's and mine for many years.

This is your chance to sit down with Bev as he shares warm memories and inspiring stories about his favorite hymns and gospel songs. You'll find that his love for the Lord shines through as he reflects on some of the greatest songs of our faith. The scriptural truths behind the lyrics and the devotional thoughts for each one will provide you with wonderful material for your daily quiet time.

If you would like to know more about the Billy Graham Evangelistic Association, please contact us toll-free at 1-877-247-2426 or via our Web site, www.billygraham.org. We would appreciate knowing how this book or our ministry has touched your life.

May God bless you.

Sincerely,

Franklin Graham
President

How Sweet the Sound

GEORGE BEVERLY SHEA

WITH

BETTY FREE SWANBERG

AND JEFFERY MCKENZIE

This Billy Graham Library Selection special edition is
published for the Billy Graham Evangelistic Association
by Tyndale House Publishers, Inc.

Tyndale House Publishers, Inc.
WHEATON, ILLINOIS

Published for the Billy Graham Evangelistic Association by Tyndale House Publishers, Inc.

A *Billy Graham Library Selection* designates materials that are appropriate to a well-rounded collection of quality Christian literature, including both classic and contemporary reading and reference materials.

TYNDALE is a registered trademark of Tyndale House Publishers, Inc.

The Tyndale quill logo is a trademark of Tyndale House Publishers, Inc.

Visit Tyndale's exciting Web site at www.tyndale.com

The memories recorded in this book are based on original interviews with George Beverly Shea by Jeffery McKenzie and Betty Free Swanberg, and on original written text from Mr. Shea. The devotional interludes are by Betty Free Swanberg as approved by Mr. Shea.

Contributing writer: Betty Free Swanberg

Edited by Lisa A. Jackson

Designed by Ron Kaufmann and Julie Chen

The primary source for the wording, punctuation, and order of stanzas is *The One Year Book of Hymns* copyright © 1995 by Robert K. Brown and Mark R. Norton, Tyndale House Publishers, Inc.

ISBN 0-8423-7042-0 (Tyndale)
ISBN 1-59328-031-9 (book with CD)
ISBN 1-59328-032-7 (book only)

Printed in the United States of America

09 08 07 06 05
7   6   5   4   3

I WOULD LIKE TO DEDICATE THIS BOOK
TO MY BELOVED KARLENE
AND MY CHILDREN, RON AND ELAINE

Table of Contents

GOSPEL SONGS, REVIVAL HYMNS, AND SPIRITUALS

SONGS SPECIAL TO THE SHEA FAMILY

A Word of Appreciation

*F*or a lifetime I have loved to *sing* "the Story of Jesus and His love." And now what a delight to *tell* the story of these songs about Him in the book, *How Sweet the Sound*. A privilege I never thought possible except now in the medium provided by this fine publisher—Tyndale House. Stories often so tender, and always spiritually uplifting.

The people at Tyndale have been most helpful, with special thanks to Jan Long Harris, Barabara Kois, Lisa Jackson, and Betty Free Swanberg, and Jeff McKenzie, a New Zealand friend now living in Nashville, who worked with me and the publisher to make this book a reality. My heartfelt thanks to my son Ron and his wife, Kathy, for their ongoing encouragement. My stepson, Steve Aceto, gave invaluable assistance in many areas during the writing of these pages.

So many in my time have been more worthy voice-wise to have joined the BGEA team, but I am so grateful that back in 1947, Billy Graham phoned and wrote me about forming a team to conduct evangelistic city-wide crusades.

It was unknown to any of us at the time that this would lead to global-wide sharing of the blessed gospel of our Lord and Savior Jesus Christ. History has been written and God's love has overshadowed these years of ministry.

I thankfully acknowledge Mr. Graham's faithful preaching of the gospel, given in the spirit of Jesus always, and now joined by his son Franklin. The music ministry as led by our beloved colleague Cliff Barrows, and his associate choir director Tom Bledsoe, has been and continues to be a blessing to the thousands of choir members and to those who have been the listeners, whether at the crusades or through the radio and television broadcasts.

I want to extend appreciation to other friends—the keyboard musicians who have been so important to all of us. I want to thank those who have given such beautiful accompaniment to the gospel songs sung by soloists from Mr. Graham's pulpit. Their

names are remembered forever: Bill Fasig, Don Hustad, John Innes, Paul Mickelson, Tedd Smith, Lorin Whitney, and the talented pianist for the first two years of the crusades, Mrs. Cliff (Billie) Barrows. Earlier in my career, there were the WMBI organ and piano accompanists—Martha French, Marybelle Robinson, and Herman Voss.

Other valuable team members who have assisted include Kerri Bruce, Kathryn Morgan, Belma Ruth Reimer, Maury Scobee, and Stephanie Wills.

In the time between crusades, there have been evenings of sacred music and song in churches and auditoriums. The musicians and accompanists have been several of those mentioned above, but also include Sharon Adams in Canada, and Susie Waldrop in North Carolina. I would like to acknowledge the composer, pianist, and producer, Kurt Kaiser. I have appreciated his beautiful music, accompaniment, and warm friendship.

Most important I want to acknowledge my precious wife Karlene. Without her help *How Sweet the Sound* would not have been written.

"My heart greatly rejoices,
And with my song I will praise Him" (Psalm 28:7, NKJV).

"And after singing a hymn they went out. . . ."
(Matthew 26:30, NASB)

Foreword

BY BILLY GRAHAM

Of all the gospel singers in the world today, the one I would rather hear more than any other is George Beverly Shea.

For over fifty years George Beverly Shea has been a faithful part of a team that has experienced the privilege of sharing the gospel of Jesus Christ around the world.

Because he has been singing hymns all his life, these songs of worship have become an integral part of who George Beverly Shea is. The meanings and stories that surround these hymns, including how they came to be written or the lives they have touched, could not be told or expressed in a more heartfelt and passionate way than through the words of my friend Bev Shea.

During crusades around the world, people have told Bev their stories of what these hymns have meant to them. Some have told dramatic and touching stories of the hymns that have driven them to their knees, others have expressed how their faith has been renewed or sustained, and many more have shared how the words and melodies of these hymns have been an anchor for them through turbulent times. All in all, these hymns have been a powerful instrument of God to draw people closer to His Word and the saving riches therein. There are so many more stories than this book could hold, but finally some of these stories are being put in print so that God's grace in special individual circumstances can be further revealed.

There have also been many letters over the years that have come into the Billy Graham Evangelistic Association for Bev. Time and time again these letters have shared how the songs Bev has sung have become a powerful influence on the letter writers' lives. These letters continually demonstrate how God has used these songs to remind people that He is waiting for them and desiring to fill their lives with His love.

Songs can touch and open a heart to hear God when sermons and preaching may fall on deaf ears. Music is such a universal language—and God has used Bev to be an instrument to touch and enrich lives. In our crusades, it is often the singing that God uses to prepare the heart to hear the gospel of our Lord Jesus Christ. That's why these stories need to be told, for they are the stories and offerings from people who have been profoundly impacted with the message of the gospel as they have listened to the music of George Beverly Shea.

The title of Bev's song "The Wonder of It All" is a declaration of the very essence of Bev's faith—a heart overwhelmed by the grace and majesty of God.

I hope that as you read these poignant and inspiring stories, they will refresh your heart. Maybe you can identify with some of these stories and be reminded again of the love God has for you. A love so deep and costly that your Heavenly Father gave His only Son, Jesus Christ, as the ultimate sacrifice by dying on the cross for your sin. He did this for you and for all of humankind.

It is my privilege to enthusiastically recommend this book to you. I hope you enjoy reading these stories. May God richly bless you and keep you.

Billy Graham

Timeless Hymns

What a way to learn great theology! That's what comes to mind whenever I sing one of the old hymns. "And Can It Be" is like putting the doctrine of salvation to music. "Come Thou Fount of Every Blessing" is a melodic lesson in grace. No wonder good hymns make for strong faith!

—Joni Eareckson Tada

Hymns are part of my devotional life. . . . The hymns continue to inspire, instruct, and give the church a vehicle to express adoration.

—Steve Green

I Will Sing the Wondrous Story

I will sing the wondrous story
Of the Christ who died for me—
How He left His home in glory
For the cross of Calvary.

Yes, I'll sing the wondrous story
Of the Christ who died for me,
Sing it with the saints in glory,
Gathered by the crystal sea.

I was lost but Jesus found me—
Found the sheep that went astray,
Threw His loving arms around me,
Drew me back into His way.

Days of darkness still come o'er me,
Sorrow's paths I often tread;
But the Savior still is with me—
By His hand I'm safely led.

He will keep me till the river
Rolls its waters at my feet;
Then He'll bear me safely over,
Where the loved ones I shall meet.

Words: Francis H. Rowley (1854–1952)
Music: Peter P. Bilhorn (1865–1936)

*H*ow we all love to be cheered by the voices of encouragement! Reflecting back, we remember those who uplifted our spirits and were used by God for direction in our lives.

I remember back to the time when I was at radio station WMBI. We had a men's octet that traveled to New York with the president of Moody Bible Institute, Dr. Will H. Houghton. There was a great Christian gathering, with one of the finest Salvation Army bands I have ever heard playing in the first part of the service.

Coming to the close of their presentation, John Fowler, the legendary tuba player, placed his instrument on the floor. He picked up a microphone, and in his marvelous, rich basso voice began, "I will sing the wondrous story of the Christ who died for me." As Mr. Fowler paused from time to time, you could hear the band members humming quietly in the background. When Mr. Fowler came to the refrain, sung so tenderly, about "the Christ who died for me," Dr. Houghton was seen wiping tears away. We were all deeply moved.

Mother Graham—Billy Graham's mother—attended the very first of her son's meetings, held in November of 1947 at the Armory in Charlotte, North Carolina.

I will never forget hearing for the first time the beautiful singing of the congregation and choir. All too soon it was my turn. Mr. Graham had written asking that I join him and Cliff Barrows there as the soloist, singing a quiet gospel song just before the message each evening. I warmly thanked him for the invitation but mentioned that most gospel singers seemed to sing a verse or two, then paused to bring a brief sermon. Would I have to do that?

"I hope not!" said Mr. Graham with a chuckle.

"Then I'd like to come with you," I said.

The first solo was from an old hymnbook; it was "I Will Sing the Wondrous Story," a truly fitting introduction to the privilege I would have of lifting up the Savior's name in song in years to come. When things began there in Charlotte, we had no inkling of what was to come: evangelistic crusades in great stadiums here and in far-off places. Yes, coming to the microphone that first night I was more than a little nervous. But I gained confidence as I heard Mr. Graham behind me, "Bless you, Bev."

On the final chorus of "I Will Sing the Wondrous Story," I raised my voice an octave. Completing the refrain *sotto voce,* these precious words came slowly, "Sing it with the saints in glory, gathered by the crystal sea."

Mother Graham wrote to me afterwards, "This is becoming one of my very favorite hymns, sung slowly and in your bass voice. We will be thinking about you and praying for you at all the meetings as you continue to sing 'The Wondrous Story.'"

To this day I haven't forgotten Mother Graham's words of encouragement. Two or three times a year I would receive a little handwritten note from her, which I carried in my wallet for quite some time. And of course, I have Mr. John Fowler, the Salvation Army tuba player, to thank for that inspiring rendition.

DEVOTIONAL INTERLUDE

Singing about the Wonderful Story

EVERYONE WILL SHARE THE STORY OF [GOD'S] WONDERFUL GOODNESS; THEY WILL SING WITH JOY OF [HIS] RIGHTEOUS- NESS. PSALM 145:7, NLT

There are many ways to share "the wondrous story." Some speak it, some sing it, and some paint it; but God asks all of us, with His help, to live it. When we show our love for Christ through our daily activities, we are truly singing the story "with the saints in glory."

To sing the story, we need the gift of our Savior's pres- ence. Even though He is back in glory, Christ continues— through the Holy Spirit—to be with those He came to save. He takes us by the hand and leads us safely through the "days of darkness" that come now and then.

Christ is not only with us but has also remained righ- teous, just like His heavenly Father. What joy that puts into our song! As Jesus' righteousness shines through us, we can point others to the Father.

Dear God, I praise You for Scriptures and songs about Your love. Thank You for the opportunity to sing Your story through my daily living. Thank You, Jesus, for hold- ing me by the hand, especially when everything seems dark and unsafe. Keep me singing about You and Your righteousness.

Betty Free Swanberg

Jesus Whispers Peace

There is a name to me most dear,
Like sweetest music to my ear;
For when my heart is troubled, filled with fear,
Jesus whispers peace.

When grief seems more than I can bear,
My soul weighed down with heavy care,
And I am sorely tempted to despair,
Jesus whispers peace.

O that the world might hear Him speak
The word of comfort that men seek.
To all the lowly and unto the meek,
Jesus whispers peace.

Words and Music: Della M. Warren (song written in 1936)
Copyright © 1936 Word Music Inc. All rights reserved. Used by permission.

Jesus Whispers Peace

*B*erent Frizen, Billy Graham, and Ruth Bell Graham were students together at Wheaton College in the 1940s. Mr. Frizen, called Bert by his friends, was a talented and popular singer on campus, involved with several singing groups. A favorite song of Bert's mother was "Jesus Whispers Peace."

Bert went on to serve in the military during World War II and was involved in the famous Battle of the Bulge. This battle took place near the borders of Belgium, Luxembourg, and France during December 1944 and January 1945. It was the largest land battle in which United States forces participated, involving more than a million soldiers from Germany, Great Britain, and America. We are told that 180,000 were wounded, captured, or killed in this terrible battle.

→ Bert Frizen, wounded during one of the attacks, lay on the battlefield, slipping in and out of consciousness. At one point, with his eyes closed, he started singing his mother's favorite hymn as best he could. When he opened his eyes, he saw a German soldier standing over him with a drawn bayonet. Bert understood enough German to know that the soldier was saying to him, "Sing it again; sing it again." *Sing es noch einmal; sing es noch einmal.*

He continued singing this beautiful song:
"There is a name to me most dear,
Like sweetest music to my ear;
For when my heart is troubled,
   filled with fear,
Jesus whispers peace."

7

Soon he felt himself being gently lifted up in the arms of the enemy soldier, who carried him to a rock ledge where the American medics found him a short time later.

Mr. Frizen returned home and graduated from Wheaton College in 1947. After he left college, I became acquainted with him over the phone and was thrilled to hear him tell in his own words about this miracle on the battlefields of France.

Even in life's most difficult situations we can call upon Jesus to whisper peace to our hearts.

DEVOTIONAL INTERLUDE
Experiencing True Peace

YOU WILL KEEP IN PERFECT PEACE ALL WHO TRUST IN YOU,
WHOSE THOUGHTS ARE FIXED ON YOU!   ISAIAH 26:3, NLT

How wonderful to know the name of Jesus, and to know the One to whom the name belongs. That name is like music to us when we're troubled, for we know that if we call on Jesus' name, He is there to whisper His peace.

When we're "lowly" and "meek," willing to put our trust in Jesus rather than in ourselves, His peace surrounds us. He doesn't try to get our attention by shouting at us. No, He gets our attention by waiting quietly and patiently for us to focus our thoughts on Him.

As we read the Scriptures and talk to God in the solitude of our home—even if it's just in a corner where we can escape the busyness of the household—Jesus is there. We come away refreshed, ready to face our busy life, because Jesus has whispered His peace.

Thank You, Lord Jesus, for Your promise of peace. Help me to put my trust in You, for only You can offer a peace that is perfect and removes my fears. Teach me to humble myself before You and to keep my thoughts focused on You so that I can enjoy the gift of Your perfect peace.

bfs

Amazing Grace

Amazing grace! how sweet the sound—
That saved a wretch like me!
I once was lost but now am found,
Was blind but now I see.

'Twas grace that taught my heart to fear,
And grace my fears relieved;
How precious did that grace appear
The hour I first believed!

The Lord has promised good to me,
His word my hope secures;
He will my shield and portion be
As long as life endures.

Through many dangers, toils and snares
I have already come;
'Tis grace hath brought me safe thus far,
And grace will lead me home.

When we've been there ten thousand years,
Bright shining as the sun,
We've no less days to sing God's praise
Than when we'd first begun.

Words: John Newton (1725–1807)
Words, stanza 5: John P. Rees (1828–1900)
Music: "New Britain" in *Virginia Harmony,* 1831

I had the opportunity to visit the town of Olney, England, for the first time in the 1950s. This is where John Newton wrote "Amazing Grace."

John Newton began preaching at the parish church of St. Peter and St. Paul in Olney, England, sixteen years after God delivered him from a life of slave trading. Almost every week, he wrote a new hymn appropriate to the Scripture lesson for the evening service.

The little town of Olney is about forty miles from London. Since the 1950s we have had several opportunities to visit there. In the vestibule of the parish church, there is an attractive wooden plaque with the names of all the clergy from the 1700s, and, of course, John Newton's name is there. How thrilling it was to see the cedar pulpit Newton stood behind when delivering his Sunday sermon. It was on exhibit in the corner of the church.

A most moving experience was visiting John Newton's gravesite in the churchyard. Don Hustad, long-time organist and musician on our team, was with me, and together we found the tombstone in a corner of the cemetery, very close to a centuries-old stone wall. Pushing aside some of the tall grass, I discovered some engraved words on the back of the stone. As I read them aloud, Don pulled an envelope from his pocket and quickly wrote them down. Standing there we rejoiced over John Newton's powerful testimony. These are the words:

> John Newton, clerk, once an infidel and libertine,
> a servant of slaves in Africa, was by the rich mercy

of our Lord and Saviour, Jesus Christ, preserved, restored, pardoned, and appointed to preach the faith he had long labored to destroy.

Back in the United States, in an RCA recording studio, when the red light went on and the orchestra began the opening of this beautiful hymn, I quoted John Newton's declaration of a life transformed.

"Preserved, restored, pardoned, and appointed!" Words could scarcely better express the "amazing" part of grace.

Amazing grace, how sweet the sound!

Newton wrote "Amazing Grace" in 1779. Nearly two hundred years later, singer Judy Collins, taking the dusty hymnbook off the shelf, gathered a group of her Nashville friends to record the song. Breaking into the Top 20 pop charts around the world, and in some places even reaching number one, "Amazing Grace" became known to millions who were not aware of its existence or of its inclusion in hymnbooks for so many years.

About this time, I was with my colleagues Cliff Barrows and Tedd Smith in Sydney, Australia, for an annual meeting of the Church of England. There we had the privilege of visiting with Archbishop Marcus Loane. The conversation turned to the phenomenal contemporary revival of the old hymn. Suddenly the archbishop excused himself from the room and, returning in a few moments with an ancient book, said, "I find here fourteen verses of the hymn and a tender account of John Newton's wonderful story of redemption, told in such expressive poetry from his very soul." He continued, "Brother George, we have you down for three solos tomorrow; we must add a fourth—'Amazing Grace'." Turning to Tedd Smith, I said, "Let's do that in a nice low key, E-flat, all right?"

Some ten or twelve thousand were gathered on the lawn and under the trees for the open-air program the next day. As Tedd began his piano introduction to "Amazing Grace," I spoke the words found on the tombstone in Olney.

What an impact John Newton's song has had upon people of all ages as it has reached into our hearts again and again.

DEVOTIONAL INTERLUDE

God's Grace

IT IS BY GRACE YOU HAVE BEEN SAVED.   EPHESIANS 2:8, NIV

John Newton identified with King David's words in 1 Chronicles 17:16, "Who am I, O Lord God . . . that thou hast brought me hitherto?" (KJV). Those words were printed with the song "Amazing Grace" in the 1808 edition of *Olney Hymns*.

We, too, might wonder why God has brought us this far. At some point in our lives, we may have been blinded to God and His love. But God's grace has helped us recognize our blindness and has opened our eyes to see God at work in us.

How good it is to praise God in song for His grace! He is an amazing God, and He blesses us with so much more than we deserve. After ten thousand years with God in glory, our eternity will just be starting! It will be an eternity filled with songs of praise to our loving Father.

> *O Lord, who am I, that You should have blessed me so richly? Thank You for Your amazing grace, which has not only saved me, but has helped my spiritually blind eyes to see Your love. I praise You now, and I will never stop praising You—not even after ten thousand years!*

bfs

And Can It Be?

And can it be that I should gain
An interest in the Savior's blood?
Died He for me, who caused His pain?
For me, who Him to death pursued?
Amazing love! How can it be
That Thou, my Lord, shouldst die for me?

Amazing love! How can it be
That Thou, my Lord, shouldst die for me?

He left His Father's throne above,
So free, so infinite His grace!
Emptied Himself of all but love,
And bled for Adam's helpless race!
'Tis mercy all, immense and free,
For, O my God, it found out me.

'Tis mystery all! th' Immortal dies!
Who can explore His strange design?
In vain the firstborn seraph tries
To sound the depths of love divine.
'Tis mercy all! let earth adore;
Let angel minds inquire no more.

Long my imprisoned spirit lay
Fast bound in sin and nature's night.
Thine eye diffused a quickening ray;
I woke—the dungeon flamed with light!
My chains fell off, my heart was free,
I rose, went forth, and followed Thee.

No condemnation now I dread;
Jesus, and all in Him is mine;
Alive in Him, my living Head,
And clothed in righteousness divine,
Bold I approach th' eternal throne,
And claim the crown, through Christ my own.

Words: Charles Wesley (1707–1788)
Music: Thomas Campbell (1777–1844)

*I*n August of 1981, <u>Morrow Coffey Graham</u>, mother of Rev. Billy Graham, went home to be with her Lord and Savior. At the memorial service in Charlotte, North Carolina, we listened to many beautiful hymns. I had the privilege of singing the traditional "The Lord Is My Shepherd," and the congregation lifted voices in perhaps the all-time family favorite, "And Can It Be?"

What amazing comfort this old hymn gave to us all, especially as we sang the last verse:

No condemnation now I dread;
Jesus, and all in Him is mine;
Alive in Him, my living Head,
And clothed in righteousness divine,
Bold I approach th' eternal throne,
And claim the crown, through Christ my own.

Charles Wesley, the writer of this hymn, was also the beloved musician of the Methodist Church, founded by his brother John. Charles wrote over six thousand hymns. Several are well-known Christmas songs ("Come, Thou Long Expected Jesus," "Hark! the Herald Angels Sing") and Easter songs ("Christ the Lord Is Risen Today," "I Know That My Redeemer Lives," and "Jesus Christ Is Risen Today").

Charles also wrote majestic songs of worship and praise, such as "Come, Thou Almighty King," "O for a Thousand Tongues to Sing," "Rejoice, the Lord Is King," and "Ye Servants of God."

The love of God provided the focus of other Wesley hymns, including "Jesus, Lover of My Soul" and "Love Divine, All Loves Excelling," as well as "And Can It Be?"

One of the special people the Billy Graham team appreciates is Joni Eareckson Tada. A great lover of hymnology, she has coauthored a series of books and CDs titled "Great Hymns of Our Faith." One of the featured songs in Book 3 is "And Can It Be?" As Joni says, "This particular hymn is the doctrine of salvation set to music."

DEVOTIONAL INTERLUDE

God's Amazing Love

FOR GOD SO LOVED THE WORLD, THAT HE GAVE HIS ONLY
BEGOTTEN SON, THAT WHOSOEVER BELIEVETH IN HIM
SHOULD NOT PERISH, BUT HAVE EVERLASTING LIFE. FOR
GOD SENT NOT HIS SON INTO THE WORLD TO CONDEMN
THE WORLD; BUT THAT THE WORLD THROUGH HIM MIGHT
BE SAVED. JOHN 3:16-17, KJV

The words of "And Can It Be?" answer a question that may
arise when we sing "Amazing Grace": *Why does God extend
His grace to us?* It is, of course, because of His "amazing
love," described in John 3.

We can experience joy as we ponder the glorious results
of Christ's death, for we know that the cross was not the
final chapter. And because of what Jesus did as the Sinless
One taking the blame for our sins, we need have no dread
when the time comes for us to "approach th' eternal
throne." How wonderful to know that because of Christ,
we can "claim the crown" we don't deserve.

*Heavenly Father, I know I don't deserve eternal life with
You. That's why I'm so thankful to You for offering it
as a free gift, purchased when Your Son, Jesus, died for
me. Thank You, Jesus, for making me alive in You,
now and for eternity.*

bfs

Blessed Assurance

Blessed assurance, Jesus is mine!
O what a foretaste of glory divine!
Heir of salvation, purchase of God,
Born of His Spirit, washed in His blood.

This is my story, this is my song,
Praising my Savior all the day long;
This is my story, this is my song,
Praising my Savior all the day long.

Perfect submission, perfect delight!
Visions of rapture now burst on my sight;
Angels descending bring from above
Echoes of mercy, whispers of love.

Perfect submission—all is at rest,
I in my Savior am happy and blest;
Watching and waiting, looking above,
Filled with His goodness, lost in His love.

Words: Fanny J. Crosby (1820–1915)
Music: Phoebe P. Knapp (1839–1908)

Blessed Assurance

$\mathcal{M}$any years ago I visited Fanny Crosby's grave in Bridgeport, Connecticut. Mr. Charles O. Baptista, formerly with Bell and Howell, was filming *Songs of Fanny Crosby,* one of the first films on the subject of gospel hymns.

I was having a difficult time memorizing my lines, so the producer said, "Well, write them down and place them in your hat on the grass—no one will see it." But this proved not to be so, as the final version showed everything! So here in the film I'm looking down, and reading from my hat, which I'm sure may have puzzled viewers.

But what really impressed me at that cemetery was Fanny Crosby's tombstone. Only a foot and a half high, the stone simply says, "Aunt Fanny." Below is the quotation: "She hath done what she could." Her name follows, "Fanny J. Crosby," with the year of her birth and her death.

After Mary anointed Jesus with perfume, some objected to this use of the costly ointment. Jesus' words to them were the same as what is on Miss Crosby's tombstone there in Bridgeport, Connecticut.

In the same cemetery is a tall monument and statue of Little Tom Thumb. And there is an even more impressive memorial for Mr. James A. Bailey, one of the founders of Barnum & Bailey Circus. Less than one hundred feet away is this small memorial stone for Fanny Crosby, a blind musician who wrote more than eight thousand gospel songs. What truth in these words: "She hath done what she could."

Fanny Crosby never resented the fact that she couldn't

see. In fact, she once declared that if she had a choice, she would prefer to remain blind. She knew that the first face she would see someday would be the face of her Savior.

Fanny's friend Mrs. Joseph (Phoebe) Knapp composed a melody without the thought of any words. As she played it for Fanny Crosby, she asked, "What does this music say to you?" Without hesitation, Fanny responded, "It says to me, 'Blessed assurance, Jesus is mine! O what a foretaste of glory divine!' " These thoughts became the first two lines of the hymn we love so much.

Of course, this song has been heard again and again in the Billy Graham crusades.

When we first started singing "Blessed Assurance" in the 1950s, Cliff Barrows's late wife, Billie, was the pianist for the meetings. While Cliff was rehearsing with the choir one night, he asked the sopranos to go an octave higher on the last measures of the chorus. This made for a beautiful sound, and has often been repeated through the years. Now it seems that many congregations and choirs sing the ending "the Billy Graham way."

DEVOTIONAL INTERLUDE

Resting in the Assurance of God's Love

WHEN WE BROUGHT YOU THE GOOD NEWS, IT WAS NOT
ONLY WITH WORDS BUT ALSO WITH POWER, FOR THE HOLY
SPIRIT GAVE YOU FULL ASSURANCE THAT WHAT WE SAID
WAS TRUE.   1 THESSALONIANS 1:5, NLT

WE HAVE FAITH THAT ASSURES OUR SALVATION.

HEBREWS 10:39, NLT

How wonderful to have complete assurance that, yes, "Jesus
is mine!" As we sing the beautiful words of Fanny Crosby,
we echo her with our own faith, which assures us that Jesus
is our Savior. He has purchased our salvation.

In a book of hymn stories that the Billy Graham Evangelistic Association published some years back, Cliff Barrows
wrote that "Blessed Assurance" is "an ideal song of testimony." It "tells the unending peace and joy of the person
who knows that God has accepted him because of what
Jesus Christ has done on his behalf."[1]

> *My Savior, how I praise You for giving me the opportu-*
> *nity to choose salvation. You made this choice possible for*
> *me when You shed Your blood on the cross. And thank*
> *You, Father God, for the Holy Spirit. He gives me the*
> *assurance that the promise of salvation in Your Word*
> *is true.*

bfs

---

[1] Cliff Barrows and Don Hustad, eds., *Crusader Hymns and Hymn Stories* (Carol Stream, Ill:, Hope
Publishing Company, 1967).

Great Is Thy Faithfulness

Great is Thy faithfulness, O God my Father,
There is no shadow of turning with Thee;
Thou changest not, Thy compassions they fail not;
As Thou has been Thou forever wilt be.

Great is Thy faithfulness!
Great is Thy faithfulness!
Morning by morning new mercies I see;
All I have needed Thy hand hath provided—
Great is Thy faithfulness, Lord, unto me!

Summer and winter, and springtime and harvest,
Sun, moon and stars in their courses above
Join with all nature in manifold witness
To Thy great faithfulness, mercy and love.

Pardon for sin and a peace that endureth,
Thy own dear presence to cheer and to guide;
Strength for today and bright hope for tomorrow,
Blessings all mine, with ten thousand beside!

Words: Thomas O. Chisholm (1866–1960)
Music: William M. Runyan (1870–1957)
Copyright © 1923. Renewal 1951 by Hope Publishing Company, Carol Stream, IL 60188. All rights reserved. International copyright secured. Used by permission.

*I*n the fall of 1939 I moved from New York to the Chicago area to become a staff member on Moody Bible Institute's radio station, WMBI. Today this is the flagship station of the Moody Broadcasting Network (MBN).

At the Institute I met the music composer of "Great Is Thy Faithfulness," Mr. William Runyan. A tall, delightful gentleman in his seventies, Mr. Runyan taught piano and voice in the fine music department there.

We became good friends; it was an honor for me to spend time with Mr. Runyan and learn from him, for he was well-versed in hymnology. I was so pleased when he would call me at the radio department and say, "When you have an opportunity, come over. I'd like to play for you a new song I'm working on." He had great talent for writing inspiring music. This man's enthusiasm was incredible. He was always victorious and happy in the Lord.

Thomas Chisholm was born in a log cabin in Kentucky and wrote more than twelve hundred poems. In 1923, he sent the words of "Great Is Thy Faithfulness" to Mr. Runyan. Upon reading these words, Mr. Runyan knew he had received a precious message that could touch lives around the world. He prayed that God would help him compose music that was uplifting and joyous. God answered that prayer. This hymn of praise has become a great favorite with congregations everywhere.

I will never forget listening to the student body of Moody Bible Institute in Chicago—1,200 strong—singing "Great Is Thy Faithfulness" at the Monday morning chapel services back in 1939. What a sound of praise to God as they sang, "Morning by morning new mercies I see."

Cliff Barrows and I had an opportunity to meet the hymn's author, Thomas Chisholm, at a senior care center. We found him seated on a park bench and talked with him for a little while. What a dear soul! He could have been thinking about his divinely-inspired words as he sat there under the trees: "Strength for today and bright hope for tomorrow. Blessings all mine, with ten thousand beside!"

In 1954, the Billy Graham team introduced this hymn at the meetings in Great Britain. People sang it enthusiastically, with heads back and voices ringing out in praise to God.

DEVOTIONAL INTERLUDE

God's Faithfulness

BECAUSE OF THE LORD'S GREAT LOVE WE ARE NOT
CONSUMED, FOR HIS COMPASSIONS NEVER FAIL. THEY ARE
NEW EVERY MORNING; GREAT IS YOUR FAITHFULNESS.

LAMENTATIONS 3:22-23, NIV

It's not surprising that Thomas Chisholm was in his fifties
when he sent his poem "Great Is Thy Faithfulness" to
William Runyan. The message of the faithfulness of God
rings true because it was written by someone who had experienced God's mercy "morning by morning."

Seeing the many ways that God has shown His faithfulness to His children encourages all of us. When we're
young, we enjoy listening to the testimonies of older folks
regarding God's good gifts and His unfailing love. As we
grow older ourselves, we can look back and recognize that
God has been faithfully guiding us throughout our life.

This song helps us sing our thanks to God for the blessings of His pardon, peace, strength, and hope, with ten
thousand more blessings beside!

*"O God my Father," Your love has never failed me.
Through each season of my life, You have been present.
Thank You for Your faithfulness.*

bfs

27

Hiding in Thee

O safe to the Rock that is higher than I,
My soul in its conflicts and sorrows would fly;
So sinful, so weary, Thine, Thine, would I be;
Thou blest "Rock of Ages," I'm hiding in Thee.

Hiding in Thee, hiding in Thee,
Thou blest "Rock of Ages,"
I'm hiding in Thee.

In the calm of the noontide, in sorrow's lone hour,
In times when temptation casts over me its power;
In the tempests of life, on its wide, heaving sea,
Thou blest "Rock of Ages," I'm hiding in Thee.

How oft in the conflict, when pressed by the foe,
I have fled to my refuge and breathed out my woe;
How often, when trials like sea billows roll,
Have I hidden in Thee, O Thou Rock of my soul.

Words: William O. Cushing (1823–1902)
Music: Ira D. Sankey (1840–1908)

ev. William Cushing, writer of the words to "Hiding in Thee," once visited my mother's family in Canada. She was just twelve years old at that time.

Rev. Cushing was both a preacher and a singer. He came to Prescott, Ontario, a picturesque town on the mighty St. Lawrence River, to visit my grandfather. Granddad was the pastor of the local Methodist church, and Mr. Cushing was his guest preacher for a week of meetings. After returning to the United States, he wrote a letter to my mother: "It's been delightful to be with you," he said. "Your piano playing is beautiful. Thank you for accompanying me as I was rehearsing in your home."

William Cushing's "Hiding in Thee" is one of the most beautiful of the more than three hundred hymns he wrote. It's a hymn-song everybody should know. Just repeating the words over and over again always brings spiritual uplift.

I understand that Mr. Cushing wrote "Hiding in Thee" and many other hymns after he lost his voice. No longer able to preach, he continued his ministry with the gift of songwriting.

He teamed up with Ira Sankey, who composed the music for "Hiding in Thee." The two men also composed "Under His Wings," a song with a similar theme. Sankey, a prolific composer of hymn tunes, became well known as a gospel singer who traveled with evangelist Dwight L. Moody in the United States, Canada, England, and Scotland.

By the way, Moody and Sankey published and sold songbooks for use in their meetings in Great Britain, the proceeds of which were used to build Carrubbers Close Mission. Now known as Carrubbers Christian Center, this mission in downtown Edinburgh is across the street from the statue of the Scottish reformer John Knox. The mission staff continues to this day actively ministering to those who pass by.

DEVOTIONAL INTERLUDE

My Hiding Place

FROM THE ENDS OF THE EARTH I CALL TO YOU, I CALL AS MY
HEART GROWS FAINT; LEAD ME TO THE ROCK THAT IS HIGHER
THAN I. FOR YOU HAVE BEEN MY REFUGE, A STRONG TOWER
AGAINST THE FOE.   PSALM 61:2-3, NIV

What a perfect hiding place God offers us! He's not there
just to provide a temporary escape—He fills us with His
love and power so that we can go out to face our life each
day. He gives us the strength and courage we need to
continue down the path that He wants us to follow. God is
a mighty Rock, and He never leaves us.

God also comforts us through His gift of music. By
singing wonderful hymns such as this one, we are able to
recall the strength that God offers us. Through the beautiful
melody of this song, we retain in our mind and heart the
message that God wants to rescue us and keep us safe.

Thank You, my Rock of safety, for allowing me to hide in
You. Teach me to rely on Your strength to see me through
difficult hours and days. After I've received Your strength,
help me to go on serving You and living in the joy of Your
comforting presence.

bfs

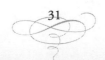

Lord, I'm Coming Home

I've wandered far away from God,
Now I'm coming home;
The paths of sin too long I've trod,
Lord, I'm coming home.

Coming home, coming home,
Nevermore to roam,
Open wide Thine arms of love,
Lord, I'm coming home.

I've wasted many precious years,
Now I'm coming home;
I now repent with bitter tears,
Lord, I'm coming home.

I've tired of sin and straying, Lord,
Now I'm coming home;
I'll trust Thy love, believe Thy word,
Lord, I'm coming home.

My soul is sick, my heart is sore,
Now I'm coming home;
My strength renew, my hope restore,
Lord, I'm coming home.

Words and Music: William J. Kirkpatrick (1838–1921)

Lord, I'm Coming Home

*Y*ears ago, while visiting a Canadian friend's home in Florida, we heard the sound of a big eighteen-wheeler coming by the window. My friend said his wife's brother was bringing a load of hay from Canada for some of the fine horses in Florida. He would soon be returning to the province of Ontario with crates of oranges for an Ottawa grocery chain.

Seeing my interest in his big red truck, the driver said, "Jump in." I told him about this being a first for me, to climb high in such a monster, never having been that close to the roaring sound of such a powerful vehicle.

Then my trucker friend told me, "It's good to see you this close. You know, driving this rig mile after mile, it gets quite tiring and lonely, especially after the sun goes down." He was quiet for a moment. Then he said, "I hear you in the dark of night as I travel down the highways, often listening to the *Hour of Decision*. I can hardly see the road after you sing songs like 'Lord, I'm Coming Home.'" His voice broke as we continued to talk about it. Then we prayed together, and I knew that a new name had been written down in Glory. It happened to my new friend from Canada, behind the steering wheel of his truck, parked in the backyard of his sister's home in Florida.

DEVOTIONAL INTERLUDE

Coming Home

SO HE RETURNED HOME TO HIS FATHER. AND WHILE HE WAS
STILL A LONG DISTANCE AWAY, HIS FATHER SAW HIM COMING.
FILLED WITH LOVE AND COMPASSION, HE RAN TO HIS SON,
EMBRACED HIM, AND KISSED HIM. . . . "QUICK! . . . WE MUST
CELEBRATE WITH A FEAST, FOR THIS SON OF MINE . . . IS
FOUND." LUKE 15:20-24, NLT

Everyone longs for the comfort and security of a loving
home. The trucker from Canada longed for a special
home—one that would be his forever. It's a home all of us
long for, even though some are not yet aware of it.

What a tender scene God paints for us in His Word
through the story of the Prodigal Son returning home to his
father's waiting arms. We're reminded of that scene when
people at a Billy Graham crusade or mission respond to the
invitation to go forward and receive Christ. Others watching
on television in the quietness of their homes, respond to
that same invitation. All of these wonderful people have
made the decision to ask God to open His "arms of love,"
and each one is saying, "Lord, I'm coming home."

*Heavenly Father, thank You for waiting for Your children
to come home. Thank You for receiving us with open
arms, never turning anyone away.*

bfs

Abide with Me

Abide with me; fast falls the eventide;
The darkness deepens; Lord, with me abide!
When other helpers fail and comforts flee,
Help of the helpless, O abide with me.

Swift to its close ebbs out life's little day;
Earth's joys grow dim; its glories pass away;
Change and decay in all around I see;
O Thou who changest not, abide with me.

I need Thy presence every passing hour;
What but Thy grace can foil the tempter's power?
Who, like Thyself, my guide and stay can be?
Through cloud and sunshine, Lord, abide with me.

I fear no foe, with Thee at hand to bless;
Ills have no weight, and tears no bitterness.
Where is death's sting? Where, grave, thy victory?
I triumph still, if Thou abide with me.

Hold Thou Thy cross before my closing eyes;
Shine through the gloom and point me to the skies;
Heaven's morning breaks, and earth's vain shadows
    flee;
In life, in death, O Lord, abide with me.

Words: Henry F. Lyte (1793–1847)
Music: William H. Monk (1823–1889)

*D*uring the years that Ruth Graham's mother, Virginia Leftwich Bell, was ill, Ruth requested that I record some of the family's favorite hymns for her. She wanted her mother's home to be filled with the beauty, wonder, and comfort that the hymns of the church bring to our hearts, especially at the time of "homegoing."

Robert Sterling and Sheldon Curry were the arrangers and conductors of the fine orchestra and choir that filled the air with glorious sounds of praise to our Lord and Savior. Mary Crowley, founder of Home Interiors and Gifts, underwrote the album as a gift to the Graham family and to the Lord. Mrs. Bell and many others received much encouragement and comfort in hours of difficulty. *Looking Homeward*[2] was the title, with an eye-catching cover photo taken by Ruth Graham from her front porch. The scene was a brilliant sunset over the Blue Ridge Mountains.

In her last illness, Ruth's mother, Mrs. Bell, received much comfort from listening to this album, perhaps especially to one of her favorites, "Abide with Me." Soon others were also playing these selections for family members in times of illness. We often hear that these hymn-songs have been a source of comfort and encouragement for many others, who like Mrs. Bell, were looking homeward, as well as for those who were with them during that difficult time.

Many of the timeless hymns were born out of tremendous suffering and trial, wherein the writers reaffirmed their own faith in the Savior and left a lasting legacy for others

---

[2]Unfortunately, this album is no longer available.

going through similar circumstances. We often learn how spiritual uplift has been given to heart and soul when someone hears or reads the words, stanza by stanza, of a hymn like "Abide with Me."

Henry Francis Lyte is said to have thought of the words for "Abide with Me" as he walked at eventide through his garden to the seaside. With failing strength, he knew that he needed "the help of the helpless." Surely the comfort of the abiding Savior was the inspiration for these words:

Who, like Thyself, my guide and stay can be?
Through cloud and sunshine, Lord, abide with me.

DEVOTIONAL INTERLUDE
Jesus' Wonderful Presence

"ABIDE WITH US, [THEY SAID,] FOR IT IS TOWARD EVENING, AND THE DAY IS FAR SPENT." LUKE 24:29, KJV

Near the end of his life, as he struggled with tuberculosis and asthma, Mr. Lyte read the Luke 24 story about the two followers of Jesus who were on their way to Emmaus. In 1847 Mr. Lyte would, of course, have read their invitation to Jesus in the King James Version: "Abide with us."

The two disciples from Emmaus didn't know at that point who Jesus was. However, after Jesus had blessed the bread and vanished, their words suggest that they were thinking, *We should have known!*

Mr. Lyte did know. You and I also know that Jesus walks with us and is pleased when we ask Him to abide with us. What better way to spend our days on this earth than to be totally aware that Jesus is walking alongside us all the way!

Lord, thank You for being my ever-present, never-changing Helper. I know that on this earth there will be clouds, but there will also be sunshine. And in it all, I will look for the light of Your presence. Lord, please abide with me forever.

bfs

O for a Thousand Tongues to Sing

O for a thousand tongues to sing
My great Redeemer's praise,
The glories of my God and King,
The triumphs of His grace!

My gracious Master and my God,
Assist me to proclaim,
To spread thro' all the earth abroad
The honors of Thy name.

Jesus! the name that charms our fears,
That bids our sorrows cease,
'Tis music in the sinners' ears;
'Tis life, and health, and peace.

He breaks the power of canceled sin,
He sets the prisoner free;
His blood can make the foulest clean;
His blood availed for me.

He speaks, and listening to His voice,
New life the dead receive;
The mournful, broken hearts rejoice;
The humble poor believe.

Hear Him, ye deaf; His praise, ye dumb,
Your loosened tongues employ;
Ye blind, behold your Savior come;
And leap, ye lame, for joy.

Words: Charles Wesley (1707–1788)
Music: Carl G. Gläser (1784–1829)

O for a Thousand Tongues to Sing

*O*for a Thousand Tongues to Sing" is the first hymn in almost every edition of the Methodist Hymnbook. The six stanzas that we usually sing, even though they are brief in length, may seem long for a hymn. Well, Charles Wesley's original poem contained three times that number!

Wesley wrote this hymn in 1739 on the first anniversary of his commitment to Christ. While he had known about Jesus from the time he was a young child, he and his brother John hadn't understood the need for personal commitment to the Lord Jesus. On the way home from a missions trip, they met a German Moravian leader, Count Nicolaus Zinzendorf, and their lives were forever changed.

Many stanzas of the song "O for a Thousand Tongues to Sing" are not included in our hymnals. It is in several of these stanzas that Charles Wesley describes his conversion experience.

Then with my heart I first believed,
Believed with faith divine.
Power with the Holy Ghost received
To call the Savior mine.

I felt my Lord's atoning blood
Close to my soul applied;
Me, me He loved, the Son of God,
For me, for me He died!

Another Moravian leader, Peter Bohler, once said, "Had I a thousand tongues, I would praise Christ Jesus with all of them." Charles Wesley used that quote as the basis for what is now the opening stanza of his hymn.

The same year that Charles wrote this poem, he and John began holding open-air revivals. It was the next year, 1740, when the original poem first appeared in a book of sacred poems.

DEVOTIONAL INTERLUDE

Singing My Redeemer's Praise

PRAISE THE LORD, O MY SOUL, AND FORGET NOT ALL HIS
BENEFITS—WHO FORGIVES ALL YOUR SINS AND HEALS ALL
YOUR DISEASES, WHO REDEEMS YOUR LIFE FROM THE PIT
AND CROWNS YOU WITH LOVE AND COMPASSION.

PSALM 103:2-4, NIV

Jesus deserves more praise than any of us could ever offer.
We wish, with Charles Wesley, that we had "a thousand
tongues" with which to sing praises to our Savior. But someday even "those who cannot speak will shout and sing"
(Isaiah 35:6, NLT). We'll gather around the throne and join
the thousands of angels who constantly give glory and praise
to the Lamb (Revelation 5:11-12).

The form of praise that pleases God the most, however, is
the praise that honors His name as we proclaim it over "all
the earth." Whether we do that through our words, by sharing our money, or by giving our time and talents, we're assisting with God's work around the globe. What a privilege!

Jesus, I praise You for who You are and for all You do.
Show me what part You want me to have in proclaiming
Your name in my home, my community, and my world.

bfs

Rock of Ages

Rock of Ages, cleft for me,
Let me hide myself in Thee;
Let the water and the blood,
From Thy wounded side which flowed,
Be of sin the double cure,
Save from wrath and make me pure.

Could my tears forever flow,
Could my zeal no languor know,
These for sin could not atone;
Thou must save, and Thou alone.
In my hand no price I bring;
Simply to Thy cross I cling.

While I draw this fleeting breath,
When my eyes shall close in death,
When I rise to worlds unknown,
And behold Thee on Thy throne,
Rock of Ages, cleft for me,
Let me hide myself in Thee.

Words: Augustus M. Toplady (1740–1778)
Music: Thomas Hastings (1784–1872)

*I*n 1984 I was in England as part of the Billy Graham crusade meetings there. During that time Cliff Barrows, George Hamilton IV, Johnny Lenning, Larry Ross, and I decided that we wanted to visit the rock that inspired Augustus Toplady to write the hymn "Rock of Ages."

Rev. Mr. Toplady, a circuit-riding preacher, had been riding his horse when suddenly the heavens opened and there commenced a terrific storm of heavy thunder and lightning. Sliding off his saddle, he found refuge and safety in the crevice of a large rock nearby.

That experience led Augustus Toplady to write, "Rock of Ages, cleft for me/Let me hide myself in Thee." How many of us, in a storm such as this, would simply be glad to be safe and dry? Rev. Toplady's thoughts, however, went directly to a spiritual application of the refuge the Lord provided for him—and further, to creating a hymn of praise.

Cliff, George, Johnny, and I found ourselves singing this beloved hymn as a quartet beside the rock. I think back on it still, remembering the faithful circuit preacher who sought refuge and then penned a hymn that has since touched millions of people around the globe.

The four of us later visited a school in the town of Cheddars (where cheddar cheese originated). Children sat on the floor around us. The teacher suggested we tell where we had been and why. Country singer George Hamilton IV, a warm Southern gentleman from Nashville's Grand Ole Opry, played his guitar and sang, to the delight of the chil-

dren. It was a joy for us as well to see happy little faces looking up at us. Their laughter and smiles said a thank-you we
will not soon forget.

While Augustus Toplady didn't live to see the worldwide impact of this hymn, we rejoice as we think about all
the people who have been blessed by this beautiful expression of faith in God.

DEVOTIONAL INTERLUDE

A Rock throughout the Ages

THE LORD IS MY ROCK, MY FORTRESS AND MY DELIVERER; MY
GOD IS MY ROCK, IN WHOM I TAKE REFUGE.   PSALM 18:2, NIV

God truly has been a Rock throughout the ages. Moses
referred to Him as a Rock (see Deuteronomy 32:4). So did
David in the Psalms.

In the New Testament we're reminded that Christ, as
part of the Trinity, has always existed. He was the spiritual
Rock of the Old Testament (1 Corinthians 10:4). But even
more than that, "the water and the blood" that flowed from
Jesus' side can save us from the wrath of God and make us
pure.

We look forward to the day when we will behold God
on His throne. Much about that day is unknown—the
details won't be revealed beforehand. But this we know:
Jesus, our "Rock of Ages," will be there; and as our Savior,
He will have hidden all of our sins.

> *Dear God, thank You for the strength and protection You
> provide. Lord Jesus, You are my Rock and my Savior. I
> praise You for being my cleft Rock throughout the eternal
> ages. "Let me hide myself in Thee."*

bfs

Safe in the Arms of Jesus

Safe in the arms of Jesus,
Safe on His gentle breast,
There by His love o'ershaded,
Sweetly my soul shall rest.
Hark! 'tis the voice of angels,
Borne in a song to me,
Over the fields of glory,
Over the jasper sea.

Safe in the arms of Jesus,
Safe on His gentle breast,
There by His love o'ershaded,
Sweetly my soul shall rest.

Safe in the arms of Jesus,
Safe from corroding care,
Safe from the world's temptations,
Sin cannot harm me there.
Free from the blight of sorrow,
Free from my doubts and fears;
Only a few more trials,
Only a few more tears!

Jesus, my heart's dear refuge,
Jesus has died for me;
Firm on the Rock of Ages,
Ever my trust shall be.
Here let me wait with patience,
Wait till the night is o'er;
Wait till I see the morning
Break on the golden shore.

Words: Fanny J. Crosby (1820–1915)
Music: William H. Doane (1832–1915)

*A*ll of my life I have loved organ music. A recent article in *The American Organist* tells us that the sound of a majestic pipe organ is "the closest we can imagine to the voice of God." Not really true, of course, but it is an arresting thought. Great organ music lends grandeur. The magazine article goes on to say, "The organ has to whisper at the same time it shakes the floor. It has to fill the room with the most wonderful sound imaginable."

When I was ready to ask our Erma's father for her hand, I said to him, "Mr. Scharfe, for a long time I've wanted to buy an old reed organ. Another desire has been to find a wife. But I think I'll let the organ go for a while." Erma's dad started to laugh. He got the point! I felt I had his permission.

Over the years I've enjoyed having several different organs in our home—different sizes, styles, and models. In 1991, I was especially privileged to receive a small pipe organ as a gift from the kind people of Manley Memorial Baptist Church in Lexington, Virginia. They were replacing it with a larger instrument. My dear friend Mr. Roy Fawcett of Winchester, Ontario, experienced in rebuilding and installing organs, made the long journey to Virginia to supervise the dismantling of one thousand pipes from the organ loft. Beautiful to behold, they are of 1926 vintage. Roy continued on to our home to do the new installation. He had become acquainted with Larry Sprinkle, former mayor of nearby Weaverville, North Carolina, also an experienced organ builder. Mr. Sprinkle and his wife, Beth Ann, came along to assist in installing the pipes in the basement and connecting them to the three-manual console upstairs.

When I was a teenager in Ottawa, I loved to play the Estey reed organ at a friend's church.

There were two teenage brothers who lived down the street from our family—Asa MacIntosh, the same age as I (fifteen at the time), and Paul, three years our senior. They were sextons for their church, taking care of cleaning on Saturday morning for the Sunday services. Asa would say to me, "Come along and play the organ while we're working."

One of the hymns they would ask for was "Safe in the Arms of Jesus." I would pull out the *vox humana* stop for the left hand, and very softly play the melody with the right hand. The music seemed to brighten the task and make the work hours go faster.

A year later, something very sad happened. Asa, at the young age of sixteen, suffered a heart attack that took his life. His mother called and said, "Asa and Paul often told me how you played the organ for them. One of the hymns they liked was 'Safe in the Arms of Jesus'. Would you play that for the service tomorrow?" The little church was crowded, and I was a little nervous because it was my first time playing before an audience. Nonetheless it was quite an honor to be able to do this as a tribute to my friend and for the family.

Many years later, in the 1960s, we were living in the Chicago area, and there was an ad in the *Chicago Tribune* for reed organs. I went to a home in the city and found organs in the living room, the basement, and the garage! Inspecting many of them, I found and bought one that looked very familiar. It was the same model as that old Estey in Ottawa. I went in search of a U-haul and took the organ home. It is still a prized possession to this day.

Arranger and composer Ralph Carmichael enjoyed hearing this story. When recording "Safe in the Arms of Jesus" at RCA, I mentioned to Ralph how I'd like to interpret the final chorus—very softly and gently. Perhaps I was thinking of Asa's service long ago. When the recording light went off in the studio in Hollywood, California—three thousand miles from Ottawa—Ralph was saying quietly, "That's a take. That's a take."

DEVOTIONAL INTERLUDE

Safety in Jesus' Arms

HE GATHERS THE LAMBS IN HIS ARMS AND CARRIES THEM
CLOSE TO HIS HEART.   ISAIAH 40:11, NIV

THEN HE TOOK THE CHILDREN INTO HIS ARMS AND PLACED
HIS HANDS ON THEIR HEADS AND BLESSED THEM.

MARK 10:16, NLT

As children, we expect to find safety in our parents' arms.
And as adults, we can continue to find safety in the arms
of Jesus. When we need to confide in someone, we know
we'll be safe in Jesus' arms as we pray, for Scripture
teaches us that "the godly run to him and are safe"
(Proverbs 18:10, NLT).

Even though evil and temptations are everywhere, we
can always run to our Savior for refuge. His strong arms
enfold us and keep out harm just as a shepherd's arms
protect his little lambs.

*Thank You, Lord, for Your open and welcoming arms.
Teach me to rest quietly on Your breast as I share my
deepest thoughts with You. Jesus, You are my Shepherd.
I feel safe when I let Your arms hold me. Give me the
patience to wait in the safety of Your arms until You
are ready to bring me to "the golden shore."*

bfs

Satisfied

All my life long I had panted
For a drink from some clear spring,
That I hoped would quench the burning
Of the thirst I felt within.

Hallelujah! I have found Him
Whom my soul so long has craved!
Jesus satisfies my longings,
Through His blood I now am saved.

Feeding on the husks around me,
Till my strength was almost gone,
Longed my soul for something better,
Only still to hunger on.

Poor I was, and sought for riches,
Something that would satisfy,
But the dust I gathered 'round me
Only mocked my soul's sad cry.

Well of water, ever springing,
Bread of life so rich and free,
Untold wealth that never faileth,
My Redeemer is to me.

Words: Clara T. Williams (1858–1937)
Music: Ralph E. Hudson (1843–1901)

$\mathcal{W}$hen I was a young lad, our family moved from Winchester, near Ottawa (in Ontario, Canada) to Houghton, New York. The older children were able to attend what was then an academy, later to become Houghton College. While we lived there, my father took trips into Western Canada to start two new churches—one in Medicine Hat, Alberta, and the other in Eyebrow, Saskatchewan.

I was eight when we moved to Houghton. One day I was walking down the main street with my father when he said to me, "Someone is coming toward us, an elderly lady I want you to meet. She is Mrs. Clara Tear Williams. She wrote number 368 in our hymnal, 'All My Life Long.'"

Even at the age of eight, I was thrilled and in awe of meeting a hymn writer. To think of being introduced to a person who wrote one of the hymns we loved to sing on Sunday mornings! We talked for only a few minutes. Later, when I would see her in church, I would look at her and say to myself, *She is a hymn writer!* I think my parents were surprised at how excited I was to meet this lady (especially since none of us knew that years later I would go on to record Mrs. Williams's hymn for RCA Victor). We didn't realize that this was perhaps a foreshadowing of what was down the road for me. I began to leaf through the hymns during Dad's sermons on Sunday mornings. The rustle of the pages might have been a little distracting, but I know he forgave me.

Satisfied to Have Found Jesus

HE SATISFIES THE THIRSTY AND FILLS THE HUNGRY WITH
GOOD THINGS.   PSALM 107:9, NLT

There is nothing like a cold drink of water to make us feel
refreshed and ready for the next task. And there is nothing
like a satisfying meal to make us feel contented at the end of
a long, hard day. But, oh, how much more satisfied we are
when we fellowship with the Lord of the universe, drinking
His Living Water and eating the Bread of Life!

It's magnificent to have a Savior who not only satisfies
every longing, but who does this beyond our expectations.
That's good news we can all share! The woman at the well,
whose story is told in John 4, knew that finding Jesus is
worth talking about. The 100 percent satisfaction that Jesus
gives is something worth describing to the people in our
neighborhoods, communities, towns, and cities.

> *Lord, no one can satisfy my deepest longings the way You
> do. You provide what I need for my physical body and for
> my spiritual soul, so I praise You for caring about every
> aspect of my being. Help me to honor You with my praise
> and to share with others the satisfaction You offer.*

bfs

So This Is Life

So this is life, this world with all its pleasures;
Struggles and tears, a smile, a frown, a sigh;
Friendship so true and love of kin and neighbor,
Sometimes it's hard to live, always to die.

The world moves on, so rapidly the living,
The forms of those who disappear replace,
And each one dreams that he will be enduring.
How soon that one becomes the missing face.

Help me to know the value of these hours;
Help me the folly of all waste to see.
Help me to trust the Christ who bore my sorrows
And thus to yield to life or death for Thee.

In all my days be glorified, Lord Jesus.
In all my ways guide me with Thine own eye.
Just where and as Thou wilt use me, Lord Jesus,
And then for me 'tis Christ to live or die.

Words: Dr. Will H. Houghton (1887–1947)
Music: George Schuler (1882–1973)
Owned by Moody Bible Institute

*W*hen I listen to this song, I think of missionaries who heard God's call and followed His voice. Dr. Will H. Houghton wrote the words just after hearing of the martyrdom of John and Betty Stam.

John studied at Moody Bible Institute, where his heart became burdened for the people of China. While preparing himself for mission work in that land, he attended a weekly prayer meeting where he met his future wife, Betty Scott, who also had her heart set on China.

Betty went to China first, in 1932, and John followed shortly after that. They were married and had a daughter, Helen, in 1934.

In that land, Communists falsely accused John and Betty of stirring up rebellion. They were executed on December 8, 1934, when only in their twenties. A Chinese pastor and his wife brought the Stams' little daughter, Helen Priscilla, to safety.

I had the privilege of knowing John's father, Peter Stam, Sr. He started and sustained the Star of Hope Mission in Patterson, New Jersey. Many great Bible scholars came to speak at this fine teaching center. At the age of twenty-seven I was invited by this patriarch of the Stam family to sing at the mission.

At the end of the service, Mr. Stam said, "It was nice to have you here; we would like to give you a gift from our bookstore." He presented to me the metal plaque that still hangs above the mantel on our fireplace. It reads:

Christ is the head of this house,
The unseen guest at every meal,
The silent listener to every conversation.

This is also a reminder of the rich history of faithful service this family has had through the generations.

Finding Life

WHILE WE LIVE, WE LIVE TO PLEASE THE LORD. AND WHEN WE DIE, WE GO TO BE WITH THE LORD. SO IN LIFE AND IN DEATH, WE BELONG TO THE LORD.   ROMANS 14:8, NLT

FOR TO ME TO LIVE IS CHRIST, AND TO DIE IS GAIN.
PHILIPPIANS 1:21, KJV

Missionaries throughout the ages, like the apostle Paul, John and Betty Stam, and Martin Burnham, have all known the truth that Christ is the reason for living and for dying. They lived to please God; and when they died, they went to be with Him.

All of us as Christians have been called to die to our sinful selves. Paul testifies in Galatians 2:20: "I no longer live, but Christ lives in me" (NIV). As we let the Lord guide us with His very "own eye," some of us may be called to serve as missionaries in our homes and communities. Others may be sent to faraway places—some of them dangerous. One may become a "missing face," going ahead of the rest of us to gain the life we all look forward to enjoying some day.

> *Lord, it is difficult when someone we love becomes a "missing face," even if that person dies in Your service. Teach us to trust You in life and in death.*

bfs

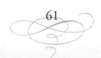

Take My Life and Let It Be

Take my life and let it be
Consecrated, Lord, to Thee;
Take my moments and my days—
Let them flow in ceaseless praise,
Let them flow in ceaseless praise.

Take my hands and let them move
At the impulse of Thy love;
Take my feet and let them be
Swift and beautiful for Thee,
Swift and beautiful for Thee.

Take my voice and let me sing
Always, only, for my King;
Take my lips and let them be
Filled with messages from Thee,
Filled with messages from Thee.

Take my silver and my gold—
Not a mite would I withhold;
Take my intellect and use
Ev'ry pow'r as Thou shalt choose,
Ev'ry pow'r as Thou shalt choose.

Take my will and make it Thine—
It shall be no longer mine;
Take my heart—it is Thine own,
It shall be Thy royal throne,
It shall be Thy royal throne.

Take my love—my Lord, I pour
At Thy feet its treasure store;
Take myself—and I will be
Ever, only, all for Thee,
Ever, only, all for Thee.

Words: Frances R. Havergal (1836–1879)
Music: Henry A. César Malan (1787–1864)

I remember singing this song with the congregation in my dad's church when I was a teenager. I'd come to the words, "Take my voice and let me sing/Always, only, for my King," and I'd think, *That's it, Lord!*

The people in Dad's congregation in Winchester, Ontario, were great singers. With songbooks in hand, they would lift their heads high and really sing!

As a pastor, what Dad received for living expenses for such a large family was limited; but he knew it was all the people could afford. He often told us, with a chuckle, about some of his experiences in the first year of his preaching.

One day he was called to a farm to officiate at his first marriage ceremony. After Dad pronounced the couple man and wife, the groom said to him, "I think I should show my appreciation and pay you for this. Please follow me." They made a long trip to the garden, where the farmer said, "Pick out the largest turnip you can find." Dad lifted a heavy one to his arms. Mother said it seemed like she ate turnip for a year.

My father loved the people of Winchester, preaching there for twenty years. The best gift he could give them was to share the gospel of our Lord Jesus Christ from his pulpit and through his quiet witness.

Mother would smile when she sang, "Take my silver and my gold"! Whenever the larder was empty she would pray about it. It seemed that soon there would be an envelope with a gift of some money in it or a basket of food placed by kind friends at the door. We kids might look up and say,

"Mom, you're wonderful." She would reply, "No, our loving God is wonderful."

In 2002, I returned to Winchester, Ontario, and participated in a Sunday afternoon concert being held in the town exhibition center. On my way to the platform, I stopped to speak to an elderly lady in a wheelchair. I reached for her hand as she said, "I'm 102 years of age and I met your father before I learned to talk. As a small baby I was christened in his arms!" What an honor to meet this dear lady.

"Take my voice and let me sing/Always, only, for my King." I see that sentence in our family room every day. It's on a plaque given to us by Kurt and Pat Kaiser from a work of calligraphy by Timothy Botts.

Frances Havergal, who wrote the words to "Take My Life and Let It Be," was an English poetess living at the same time as the blind hymn writer Fanny Crosby. They admired each other's work but never met.

Even though Miss Havergal had poor health, her short life was totally consecrated to God. She was talented musically—in voice and piano—and her goal in life was to serve the Lord. She did whatever she could to help others, spiritually and physically.

Toward the end of her life, after writing "Take My Life and Let It Be," Miss Havergal gathered together the jewels she had acquired and sent them to The Missionary House, where they could be disposed of and used for God's kingdom. She wrote to a friend that she had never before found such enjoyment in giving.

Giving All to Jesus

"IF ANY OF YOU WANTS TO BE MY FOLLOWER," [JESUS] TOLD THEM, "YOU MUST . . . FOLLOW ME. IF YOU TRY TO KEEP YOUR LIFE FOR YOURSELF, YOU WILL LOSE IT. BUT IF YOU GIVE UP YOUR LIFE FOR MY SAKE AND FOR THE SAKE OF THE GOOD NEWS, YOU WILL FIND TRUE LIFE." MARK 8:34-35, NLT

What a perfect daily prayer of commitment Frances Havergal's words can become for every Christian. If we want to offer our whole life to Christ, we need to tell Him to take our hands, our feet, our voice, our lips, our resources, our mind, our will, our heart, and our love. That covers all of our life quite well.

What a joy it is to offer all of ourselves to the Lord! When we tell Him, "Take myself—and I will be/Ever, only, all for Thee," we're surrendering everything to Christ. He responds by giving us total peace in Him, and that's more than a fair exchange.

> *Lord, I sing this song for You now. Take all of my life and consecrate it for Your service. Thank You for the "true life" You give back to me when I give up my life. I want to turn away from all selfish ambition to follow You.*

bfs

The Old Rugged Cross

On a hill far away stood an old rugged cross,
The emblem of suffering and shame;
And I love that old cross where the dearest and best
For a world of lost sinners was slain.

So I'll cherish the old rugged cross,
'Til my trophies at last I lay down;
I will cling to the old rugged cross,
And exchange it some day for a crown.

O that old rugged cross, so despised by the world,
Has a wondrous attraction for me;
For the dear Lamb of God left His glory above
To bear it to dark Calvary.

In the old rugged cross, stained with blood so
    divine,
A wondrous beauty I see;
For 'twas on that old cross Jesus suffered and died
To pardon and sanctify me.

To the old rugged cross I will ever be true,
Its shame and reproach gladly bear;
Then He'll call me some day to my home far away,
Where His glory forever I'll share.

Words and Music: George Bennard (1873–1958)

*W*hen I was five years of age, there was an incident at our home in Winchester, Ontario, that my parents liked to recall, especially later when one of their sons became a gospel singer. One Saturday morning we heard a knock at the door. Standing there were two gentlemen who planned to hold evangelistic services at our church. Knowing Mother to be a fine pianist, they asked her to help them learn a song they said was new: "The Old Rugged Cross." They wished to sing it as a duet in the morning service. My parents would later tell how I stood by the piano, with mouth wide open, listening to the voices of those wonderful singers! Oh, yes. Since that time, millions of people have grown to love "The Old Rugged Cross."

I met the composer of the words and music, Rev. George Bennard, in 1940 at a Bible conference in Cedar Lake, Indiana. During a remote broadcast there for radio station WMBI Chicago, I was the station's announcer for the week. What a joy to visit with the composer of "The Old Rugged Cross." Rev. Bennard told us he was the son of a coal miner and would have followed in his father's footsteps had he not been called to become a minister and evangelist.

Asked how he came to write "The Old Rugged Cross," George Bennard told how he was thinking of the cross of Jesus one day. He had been composing music at the piano, and his mind seemed to want to dwell on the death of Christ. Then words came, an inspired answer to his own spiritual quest.

Several midwestern towns claim to be the home of "The Old Rugged Cross." It appears that Rev. Bennard wrote the words in Albion, Michigan, a town that now has a historical marker identifying it as the birthplace of the beloved gospel hymn. It was introduced at a revival meeting in a church in Pokagon, Michigan. The old church, which originally served as a barn, is now being restored.

What really started "The Old Rugged Cross" on its way to becoming well-known was a large convention of evangelists gathering in Chicago. Hearing this song for the first time, these delegates carried the melody and lyrics with them back to their homes all over the country. It must be said that Homer Rodeheaver, choir director and soloist for the Billy Sunday meetings, also had a large part in making this beautiful hymn known far and wide.

In 1998, there was an eighty-fifth anniversary celebration in Michigan for what is said to be the best loved of all twentieth-century hymns. Musical performances included choirs representing Indian, Russian, Korean, and West African churches. In San Diego in 2003, I had the privilege of singing this wonderful hymn of faith to an audience of fifty-four thousand people before Mr. Graham's message on John 3:16. I shall never forget the volunteer choir of some six thousand voices that joined in on the final chorus.

So I'll cherish "The Old Rugged Cross."

DEVOTIONAL INTERLUDE

Cherishing the Cross

GOD FORBID THAT I SHOULD GLORY, SAVE IN THE CROSS OF
OUR LORD JESUS CHRIST.   GALATIANS 6:14, KJV

If we ever have any doubts about Jesus' love, all we need to
do is recall His willingness to leave "His glory above." He
did this, knowing He would face a "dark Calvary" for you
and for me. When we cherish the cross, what's most important is cherishing the One who gave His life for us on that
old cross because He loved us so much.

The true beauty of the cross is visible only in the divine
bloodstains of Jesus described in the third stanza of this
song. Even though Jesus knew He would have to endure the
cross, He also understood the joy that would follow. One
day He will be seated beside God the Father, welcoming
those for whom He died (Hebrews 12:2).

> *How I praise You, Jesus, for the unselfish love that took*
> *You to the cross. You are the greatest treasure of all, and*
> *I cherish You. When I look at the cross, help me to see*
> *Your beauty. You are the Lamb of God, whose sacrifice*
> *pardons and cleanses me. I look forward to seeing You*
> *when You will be seated beside God the Father,*
> *welcoming me!*

bfs

There Is a Green Hill Far Away

There is a green hill far away,
Without a city wall,
Where the dear Lord was crucified,
Who died to save us all.

Oh, dearly, dearly has He loved,
And we must love Him too,
And trust in His redeeming blood,
And try His works to do.

We may not know, we cannot tell
What pains He had to bear;
But we believe it was for us
He hung and suffered there.

He died that we might be forgiv'n,
He died to make us good,
That we might go at last to heav'n,
Saved by His precious blood.

There was no other good enough
To pay the price of sin;
He only could unlock the gate
Of heav'n, and let us in.

Words: Cecil F. Alexander (1818–1895)
Music: George C. Stebbins (1846–1945)

There Is a Green Hill Far Away

*D*uring the time I served on the music and announcing staff for the Moody Bible radio station, WMBI, in Chicago, I took a leave of absence in the summer of 1943. Jack Wyrtzen, the founder of Word of Life Fellowship, asked me to spend the summer with him in his ministry in New York. His regular soloist, tenor Carlton Booth, was taking the summer off.

One day we drove to the nearby Catskill Mountains in New York State to visit the well-known hymn writer, George C. Stebbins. I was thrilled! Mr. Stebbins had written the music for several hymns, including "Saved by Grace," "There Is a Green Hill Far Away," and Fanny Crosby's "Jesus Is Tenderly Calling You Home."

We visited the cottage where a niece of Mr. Stebbins was caring for him. Mr. Stebbins, then ninety-five years of age, stood six-feet-three-inches tall and had such a pleasant, deep speaking voice. What a gracious, gentle man.

I told him how much I enjoyed "There Is a Green Hill Far Away." He had composed the music, and Cecil Alexander had written the words. Most of Cecil's writing was for children. Her goal was to give children truths of the Christian faith in simple words that they could easily understand.

As the time of our visit was coming to a close, Jack asked me to sing for Mr. Stebbins. Knowing he was not able to hear very well, I stepped closer and sang a verse of "There Is a Green Hill Far Away." Mr. Stebbins said in his bass voice, "You sound just like Carlton Booth!" Jack and I tried to hide our smiles; our friend Carlton's voice was in fact a very high tenor. Nonetheless, the compliment was warmly appreciated.

Mr. Stebbins gave me a book, *Reminiscences and Gospel Hymn Stories.* I offered him my new Waterman fountain pen to use in signing it. He took it and wrote inside the front cover, with trembling hand, "George C. Stebbins to my new friend George B. Shea." I was delighted! Then he asked if he could keep the pen! This wonderful hymn writer, who lived to be almost one hundred years old, received my pen as a gift, but I felt that I had obtained a far greater gift—a rare and beautiful one—the privilege of being with a hymn writer who touched so many lives around the world with his music.

Oh, dearly, dearly has He loved,
And we must love Him too,
And trust in His redeeming blood,
And try His works to do.

DEVOTIONAL INTERLUDE

Thankful for the Hill

THEY TOOK JESUS AND LED HIM AWAY. CARRYING THE CROSS
BY HIMSELF, JESUS WENT TO THE PLACE CALLED SKULL HILL
(IN HEBREW, *Golgotha*). THERE THEY CRUCIFIED HIM.

JOHN 19:16-18, NLT

Every biblical city had walls around it for protection. But
Jesus was taken to a hill, far from the safety of a city
surrounded by walls. He had to carry His cross outside of
Jerusalem to Golgotha, where He was crucified.

How could anyone be "good enough to pay the price of
sin"? No mere human could have filled that role. But Jesus
Christ, who "existed before everything else began" and
"holds all creation together" (Colossians 1:17, NLT), *was*
good enough. "For God in all his fullness was pleased to live
in Christ, and by him God reconciled everything to himself.
He made peace with everything in heaven and on earth by
means of his blood on the cross" (Colossians 1:19-20).

We are so thankful when we're able to experience love
on a human level. But how much greater the love we're
allowed to share with our Creator and Savior!

*Dear Lord, thank You for loving me and allowing me to
return Your love. I know that no one else could "unlock
the gate of heav'n" for me.*

bfs

What a Friend We Have in Jesus

What a Friend we have in Jesus,
All our sins and griefs to bear!
What a privilege to carry
Everything to God in prayer!
O what peace we often forfeit,
O what needless pain we bear,
All because we do not carry
Everything to God in prayer!

Have we trials and temptations?
Is there trouble anywhere?
We should never be discouraged,
Take it to the Lord in prayer.
Can we find a friend so faithful
Who will all our sorrows share?
Jesus knows our every weakness,
Take it to the Lord in prayer.

Are we weak and heavy-laden,
Cumbered with a load of care?
Precious Savior, still our refuge—
Take it to the Lord in prayer.
Do thy friends despise, forsake thee?
Take it to the Lord in prayer;
In His arms He'll take and shield thee,
Thou wilt find a solace there.

Words: Joseph M. Scriven (1819–1886)
Music: Charles C. Converse (1834–1918)

What a Friend We Have in Jesus

I applied for my driver's license as a boy of fourteen in Ottawa. As the test began, I said to the examiner, "You have a very famous name, sir. It was Joseph Scriven who wrote the very beautiful hymn 'What a Friend We Have in Jesus.' " I noticed the examiner seemed very pleased to have his name associated with the beloved hymn. May I say I thought the test was over delightfully soon?

Joseph Scriven, a young man from Ireland who authored this hymn, was to be married in 1840. The night before the wedding, his bride-to-be accidentally drowned.

Moving to Canada, he became a servant to the underprivileged and physically challenged. Again wedding plans ended with the illness and death of his second fiancé.

Despite a life of hardship and illness, Mr. Scriven wrote this hymn-song as his testimony. Even though we go through difficult trials and grief, Jesus is our Friend, a very present help in times of trouble.

In Port Hope, Ontario, a monument was erected in a tribute to Joseph Scriven, the Irish immigrant who was a friend to many and who found a friend in Jesus.

In February of 1953, after Dwight D. Eisenhower had just become president, he asked for prayer support from Senator Frank Carlson and Billy Graham. That year, many members of the House and Senate came together for a combined prayer breakfast. These national leaders gathered with the president to pray, to seek God's guidance, and to express their dependence on Him. Mr. Graham has attended most of these breakfasts over the years.

I remember staying in a Washington hotel in 1954 and attending the prayer breakfast. I was seated next to my friend Russell Hitt, who later became editor of *Eternity* magazine. Soon he was asking, "Are you singing this morning?"

"Oh, no, Russ, I'm just here to listen." We were served plates of toast with bacon and eggs.

Before long I felt a hand on my shoulder. It was Abraham Vereide, the gentleman who had been instrumental in organizing the prayer breakfast movement. He said, "My friend, would you come up with me and sing the president's favorite hymn, 'What a Friend We Have in Jesus'?"

Now what was I going to do? I had just finished eating soft eggs, a singer's nemesis. In almost the next minute I was at the microphone, saying to the audience, "If you'd like to sing along, please do."

The next day, back home in Illinois, I turned on *The Today Show* and was so surprised to see the president standing next to me, singing along with all of us:

O what peace we often forfeit,
O what needless pain we bear,
All because we do not carry
Everything to God in prayer!

Friendship with Jesus

JESUS SAID, "COME TO ME, ALL OF YOU WHO ARE WEARY AND CARRY HEAVY BURDENS, AND I WILL GIVE YOU REST."

MATTHEW 11:28, NLT

I HAVE CALLED YOU FRIENDS.   JOHN 15:15, KJV

Joseph Scriven, who had experienced so much sorrow throughout his life, wrote the words for "What a Friend We Have in Jesus" to send to his ill mother in Ireland. What better advice could anyone give to a family member or friend in need of love, healing, or comfort?

How wonderful it is to know that we can come to God through His Son, Jesus, when we are weary and have heavy burdens. We experience so much peace and joy when we tell God about everything in our prayers.

No one escapes "trials and temptations." But we can say, "Why am I discouraged? Why so sad? I will put my hope in God! I will praise him again—my Savior and my God!" (Psalm 42:5-6, NLT).

Thank You, Jesus, for being my Friend and for always listening to my cares. You bless me by sharing my load with me. I praise You, my Savior, for being my "shield" and "solace"—and the most wonderful Friend of all.

bfs

Yes, There Is Comfort

Is there no comfort for sorrow,
Nothing but heartaches and tears?
Is there no sunshine tomorrow,
Nothing but darkness and fears?

Yes, there is comfort for sorrow,
There's rest for the weariest heart.
And, praise God, there'll be sunrise tomorrow;
He'll return, and He'll never depart.

Is there no cure for our troubles,
Nothing but failure and loss?
Are they, our pleasures, but bubbles?
Are all our treasures but dross?

Must we continually stumble?
Will nothing precious remain?
Is all we've built meant to crumble?
Are all our efforts in vain?

Words: Kaleb Johnson
Music: Sven Ahlven

*M*any of the old hymns and gospel songs are indeed timeless.

Three days after the horrendous tragedy of September 11, 2001, I was scheduled to sing a few songs at Conover, North Carolina, in a mission—a crusade—with the Reverend Ralph Bell, from the Billy Graham team. Some fifteen thousand people had gathered there for the evening outdoor service. Of course everyone was thinking about the terrible events in New York, Washington, and Pennsylvania.

As I walked to the podium and picked up the microphone, I knew that everyone was still thinking about what happened three days earlier. Without even introducing the song, I sang,

> *Is there no comfort for sorrow?*
> *. . . Will nothing precious remain?*
> *Is all we've built meant to crumble?*
> *Are all our efforts in vain?*

Then the music soars as the chorus answers the questions:

> *Yes, there is comfort for sorrow,*
> *There's rest for the weariest heart.*
> *And, praise God, there'll be sunrise tomorrow;*
> *Christ will return, and He'll never depart.*

This song not only tells of the return of our Lord, but also speaks to the more difficult events of life.

The music for "Yes, There Is Comfort" was written by a friend of mine. NBC in Chicago had quite an orchestra in the forties. Victor Hedgren was an arranger for their orchestra. When he wrote songs of faith, he used the pen name Sven Ahlven.

For the evangelistic mission that September night in 2001, Ralph Bell was unable to fly in because of the tragedy that had just occurred. North Carolina congressman Robin Hayes agreed to substitute for him. It was wonderful to hear this public leader speak from a position of faith, bringing a message of hope in Christ at such a time as this.

⁓⁓

DEVOTIONAL INTERLUDE

God's Comfort

PRAISE BE TO THE GOD AND FATHER OF OUR LORD JESUS CHRIST, THE FATHER OF COMPASSION AND THE GOD OF ALL COMFORT. 2 CORINTHIANS 1:3, NIV

After one September day, it seemed that "nothing precious" would remain. Yet in spite of the devastation, there is a promise that does remain—the promise of "rest for the weariest heart."

This song dramatically portrays the change that takes place in our heart when we allow God to bless us with His comfort. No one but God can take tears of sorrow and turn them into joyous sunshine. His presence through the dark nights gives us the confidence to believe that one day He will bring a sunrise that will never set.

The melody of this song can make a heart soar. Our soul is refreshed as we sing, "Praise God, there'll be sunrise tomorrow!"

Heavenly Father, thank You for being the "God of all comfort" and for promising rest to my weary heart. I know that You stay with me even when everything around me crumbles. Teach me, Father, to tell You how I feel when my heart is weary, and to praise You for the promise of Your return, when You will "never depart!"

bfs

Gospel Songs, Revival Hymns, and Spirituals

People respond to heart songs. . . . Melody, which comes
from within, has an even deeper level of communication
than the spoken word. . . . You can communicate spiritual
truth through music in ways that will be remembered.

—CLIFF BARROWS

His Eye Is on the Sparrow

Why should I feel discouraged,
Why should the shadows come,
Why should my heart be lonely,
And long for heav'n and home,
When Jesus is my portion?
My constant friend is He:
His eye is on the sparrow,
And I know He watches me;
His eye is on the sparrow,
And I know He watches me.

I sing because I'm happy,
I sing because I'm free,
For His eye is on the sparrow,
And I know He watches me.

"Let not your heart be troubled,"
His tender word I hear,
And resting on His goodness,
I lose my doubts and fears;
Though by the path He leadeth,
But one step I may see;
His eye is on the sparrow,
And I know He watches me;
His eye is on the sparrow,
And I know He watches me.

Whenever I am tempted,
Whenever clouds arise,
When song gives place to sighing,
When hope within me dies,
I draw the closer to Him,
From care He sets me free;
His eye is on the sparrow,
And I know He watches me;
His eye is on the sparrow,
And I know He watches me.

Words: Civilla D. Martin (1866–1948)
Music: Charles H. Gabriel (1856–1932)

*I*n the 1950s, Ethel Waters was performing the lead role
in the famous New York Broadway play "The Member of the
Wedding." After the show came to an end, Ethel heard about
the Billy Graham Crusade at Madison Square Garden. She
loved Mr. Graham's preaching and hearing the two thou-
sand-voice choir. One of the team members, Lane Adams,
recognized her as she stood in line, waiting to go inside. He
said, "Ethel, it's good to see you. Would you like to sing in
the choir? We'll save a place for you so you can join us any
night when you're able to come." She didn't miss a night in
the choir after that. Even though Ethel didn't want anyone to
know she was there, everyone in the choir knew. We loved
having her with us.

One night, Cliff asked her if the next Saturday she'd like
to sing "His Eye Is on the Sparrow," the hit song of "The
Member of the Wedding." An arrangement was written for
the choir so they could sing with her. The people loved
hearing Ethel Waters sing that beloved song, which she sang
every weekend for the next eight weeks. In the closing
moments of the song, she had the cutest little way of singing, "And I know he watches . . . *we*" as she spread her arms
open wide with a large smile on her face!

People really responded.

"The Member of the Wedding" had a long run on
Broadway. Miss Waters played a member of the household
staff with a loving, nurturing spirit—a testimony of who
Ethel was in real life. In the play the groom's young sister

didn't want her brother to leave her. She insisted on going with him on his honeymoon! Ethel's character, knowing what was happening, hugged the young girl to her and said, "It's all right, honey," and broke into song with:

Why should I feel discouraged,
Why should the shadows come,
Why should my heart be lonely . . .
His eye is on the sparrow,
And I know He watches you, honey!

One year the show went to Chicago and had a three-week run there. My family, having come to know Ethel well at the crusades, went to see her perform. We invited her to come to our home in the Chicago suburb of Western Springs. She said, "I will. After the last show is over, I'll come with you—I'll be all packed and ready to go."

It was such a joy for Erma and me to have this precious woman in our home. Our children, Ron and Elaine, grew to love her as we did.

Miss Waters sat in a chair that I still have in our basement here in North Carolina. (I call it the Ethel Waters chair.) She talked about what a contrast our home was to the life that she was exposed to in the theater and expressed how glad she was to spend time in a quieter Christian atmosphere. She went on to say it encouraged her and strengthened her faith. Having Miss Waters with us, we felt, "What a privilege, what a privilege!"

In the evening in that comfortable chair, with outstretched arms—and with such feeling she would start to sing slowly in her deep, rich contralto voice:

Since Christ my soul from sin set free,
This world has been a heaven to me.
Amid earth's sorrows and its woe,
'Tis heaven my Saviour here to know.
Oh, hallelujah—yes, 'tis heaven;
'Tis heaven to know my sins forgiv'n.
On land or sea, no matter where,
Where Jesus is, 'tis heaven there.[3]

It was beautiful.

One night in 1974 Miss Waters came to a crusade in Knoxville, Tennessee. Some 250 students at the university decided they would interrupt the meeting. They were boisterous—even while the choir was singing "The Lord's Prayer." It was disconcerting, but we knew they were young and that we needed to forgive them in our hearts. Ethel rose to sing and said, "I've been hearing a lot of racket! If I were over there, I'd be your mama and give you all a good spanking." Pausing for a moment, she gently added, "Then I'd love you." The kids quieted down!

Cliff Barrows tells about visiting Ethel several days after an earthquake shook the Los Angeles area, including the building where she had an apartment on the fifteenth floor. Cliff asked her, "What happened the other morning?" Ethel said, "Well, the bed was rocking and I was crying out, 'Dear Jesus, You know my address, and I know Yours!' "

One night in 1977 while on vacation in Canada I heard on the radio that Ethel Waters had passed away. A week

---

[3]From the song "Where Jesus Is, 'Tis Heaven." Words were written by C.F. Butler, Copyright © 1926 Hope Publishing. Renewed.

before she died, she had heard me sing "What a Friend We Have in Jesus" on a Los Angeles radio program. Ethel had requested I sing this favorite at her funeral. We left immediately for Los Angeles. It was such a privilege to be with so many of her friends, including Cliff Barrows and Grady Wilson from the Billy Graham team. Grady gave the message at the memorial service at Forest Lawn Memorial Park.

People truly loved Ethel Waters. She gave her heart to the Lord and to us, for which we are so thankful.

DEVOTIONAL INTERLUDE

God's Care for Sparrows — and for Me

NOT EVEN A SPARROW, WORTH ONLY HALF A PENNY, CAN
FALL TO THE GROUND WITHOUT YOUR FATHER KNOWING
IT. . . . SO DON'T BE AFRAID; YOU ARE MORE VALUABLE TO
HIM THAN A WHOLE FLOCK OF SPARROWS.

MATTHEW 10:29-31, NLT

How special it is to learn what Jesus said about his heavenly
Father in Matthew 10. We can be confident that His eye is
on each of *us*.

Wherever we go and whatever we do, God is watching,
leading, and caring for us. Knowing that this is true gives us
happiness and freedom worth singing about!

> *Dear Lord, You have put a song in my heart because of
> Your loving care. I know You keep Your eye on all of Your
> creation, but You have said that I am more valuable to
> You than anything else You created. Thank You for
> letting me know that. And thank You for the wonderful
> freedom Your watchful presence gives me.*

bfs

The Ninety and Nine

There were ninety and nine that safely lay
In the shelter of the fold,
But one was out on the hills away,
Far off from the gates of gold;
Away on the mountains wild and bare,
Away from the tender Shepherd's care,
Away from the tender Shepherd's care.

"Lord, Thou hast here Thy ninety and nine;
Are they not enough for Thee?"
But the Shepherd made answer: "This of Mine
Has wandered away from Me;
And although the road be rough and steep,
I go to the desert to find My sheep.
I go to the desert to find My sheep."

But none of the ransomed ever knew
How deep were the waters crossed;
Nor how dark was the night the Lord passed thro'
Ere He found His sheep that was lost.
Out in the desert He heard its cry,
Sick and helpless and ready to die;
Sick and helpless and ready to die.

"Lord, whence are those blood drops all the way
That mark out the mountain's track?"
"They were shed for one who had gone astray
Ere the Shepherd could bring him back."
"Lord, whence are Thy hands so rent and torn?"
"They are pierced tonight by many a thorn;
They are pierced tonight by many a thorn."

And all thro' the mountains, thunder riven,
And up from the rocky steep,
There arose a glad cry to the gate of heav'n,
"Rejoice! I have found My sheep!"
And the angels echoed around the throne,
"Rejoice, for the Lord brings back His own!
Rejoice, for the Lord brings back His own!"

Words: Elizabeth C. Clephane (1830–1869)
Music: Ira D. Sankey (1840–1908)

I love to tell the story of how this song was written. It's a story about Dwight L. Moody and Ira D. Sankey, and how God used the two of them as they ministered together in England and Scotland.

In 1874, Mr. Moody and Mr. Sankey were traveling by train on a short trip from Glasgow to Edinburgh for a service one evening. Mr. Sankey was reading a newspaper and noted Elizabeth Clephane's poem on the editorial page. He handed it to Mr. Moody, who seemed to pay little attention and soon returned it to him without comment.

However, Dwight L. Moody, the great evangelist, must have been impressed by the poem. That evening as Mr. Moody began his sermon, Sankey realized the topic had been changed to the story of the lost sheep. Coming to the close of his message, Mr. Moody said to the people, "Mr. Sankey has an appropriate song to sing." Taking the newspaper clipping from his pocket and placing it on the organ, Ira Sankey began to sing:

There were ninety and nine that safely lay
In the shelter of the fold . . .

At the end of the first verse, composing the music as he went along, he hoped he could remember the melody for the next verse! and the next! and the next! He did! That's how the beautiful hymn "The Ninety and Nine" came to gospel-song lovers everywhere.

During the 1966 Billy Graham meetings at Earl's Court

in London, Cliff Barrows and I went by train to visit the little Carrubbers Close Mission in Edinburgh. This mission was built in the center of Edinburgh and funded by the sale of the Moody-Sankey songbook prepared for their U.K. services. There we saw the little pump organ that Mr. Sankey had used in the British Isles. The mission was being renovated, so the mission staff decided to crate the organ and send it as a gift to the Billy Graham Evangelistic Association in Minneapolis. This organ has been in the chapel there for over thirty years and now will reside in the new Billy Graham headquarters in Charlotte, North Carolina.

Can you imagine the joy it was for me to play, sing, and record "The Ninety and Nine" on this very same pump organ? From this recording, a square plastic record, in the old 78-rpm format, was made available by request.

Many hearts have been blessed by the tender message of "The Ninety and Nine" and the story of its origin.

The Shepherd's Care

IF A SHEPHERD HAS ONE HUNDRED SHEEP, AND ONE
WANDERS AWAY AND IS LOST, WHAT WILL HE DO? WON'T HE
LEAVE THE NINETY-NINE OTHERS AND GO OUT INTO THE
HILLS TO SEARCH FOR THE LOST ONE? AND IF HE FINDS IT,
HE WILL SURELY REJOICE OVER IT MORE THAN OVER THE
NINETY-NINE THAT DIDN'T WANDER AWAY! IN THE SAME
WAY, IT IS NOT MY HEAVENLY FATHER'S WILL THAT EVEN ONE
OF THESE LITTLE ONES SHOULD PERISH.

MATTHEW 18:12-14, NLT

The parable of the lost sheep is such a tender description of
our Savior's love. Long before we ever made a commitment
to Him, He was searching for us.

How important are we to Jesus? In a crowd of
ninety-nine, He knows if we're missing. No mountain is too
high to keep Him from rescuing us. The anguish of the
Cross did not prevent Him from dying to save us.

I am so thankful, Lord, that not one little lamb is insig-
nificant to You. And I am grateful that You searched for
even me and found me. I pray for all who have said yes to
Your voice. May we always follow closely behind You.

bfs

The Love of God

The love of God is greater far
Than tongue or pen can ever tell;
It goes beyond the highest star,
And reaches to the lowest hell.
The guilty pair, bowed down with care,
God gave His Son to win;
His erring child He reconciled,
And pardoned from his sin.

Oh, love of God, how rich and pure!
How measureless and strong!
It shall forevermore endure—
The saints' and angels' song.

When hoary time shall pass away,
And earthly thrones and kingdoms fall;
When men who here refuse to pray,
On rocks and hills and mountains call;
God's love, so sure, shall still endure,
All measureless and strong;
Redeeming grace to Adam's race—
The saints' and angels' song.

Could we with ink the ocean fill,
And were the skies of parchment made;
Were ev'ry stalk on earth a quill,
And ev'ry man a scribe by trade;
To write the love of God above
Would drain the ocean dry;
Nor could the scroll contain the whole,
Tho' stretched from sky to sky.

Words and Music: Frederick M. Lehman (1868–1953)
Words, stanza 3: Unknown

*W*hile pastoring several small congregations, the Reverend Frederick M. Lehman needed to augment his income by seeking other employment at a local cheese factory. One day he found a poem hidden in the lunch his wife had prepared. She had found the poem on the editorial page of the local newspaper:

Could we with ink the ocean fill . . .

Arriving home that evening, he thanked her for the needed encouragement. Placing the poem on the old reed organ, he began to sing the words and play the music that had come to him during the day.

I have loved singing this old favorite through the years and once even received a letter from Mr. Lehman's granddaughter. She thanked me for including this song on *The Hour of Decision* radio programs, recounting the lunchbox story about the writing of this gospel song that has touched the hearts of so many over the years.

It has been said that the words of the last stanza date back to the eleventh century and are based on a Jewish poem written by a rabbi in Germany. The words were translated from the Aramaic language. Some say that later they appeared on the walls of an institution—songbooks have noted that fact for many years.

The Jewish background was confirmed to me in a conversation with a young rabbi with whom I became acquainted during the Madison Square Garden Crusade in

1957. He said he liked to attend the meetings and study Mr. Graham's oratory. One evening the rabbi asked, "Haven't you been singing a song called 'The Love of God'? The last verse is very familiar to me—the part that starts, 'Could we with ink the ocean fill . . .' " Later I received a Philadelphia newspaper clipping that said these lines were used in the Jewish ceremony The Festival of Weeks.

Whatever the origins of the third stanza, we're glad that the words inspired Mr. Lehman to write the first two stanzas and chorus of "The Love of God" and to compose the music.

It never ceases to amaze how God uses people from all walks of life and from different circumstances to bring the message of His love to the world. Lehman and the writer of the third stanza never knew each other. They lived in different times and under different circumstances. Yet they had one consuming message—God's love—which is found in this wonderful hymn-song.

DEVOTIONAL INTERLUDE

God's Gift of Love

I AM PERSUADED, THAT NEITHER DEATH, NOR LIFE, NOR ANGELS, NOR PRINCIPALITIES, NOR POWERS, NOR THINGS PRESENT, NOR THINGS TO COME, NOR HEIGHT, NOR DEPTH, NOR ANY OTHER CREATURE, SHALL BE ABLE TO SEPARATE US FROM THE LOVE OF GOD, WHICH IS IN CHRIST JESUS OUR LORD.   ROMANS 8:38-39, KJV

When God created us, He chose to love every one of us—unconditionally—no matter how we respond.

God has expressed His love for each "erring child" in so many ways. He gives us wonderful gifts, the greatest of which, of course, is the loving gift of His Son.

God's love "shall forevermore endure." Too often, we have become familiar with short-lived commitments. It's so good to read in Scripture about God's long-term commitment to His people.

Nothing on this earth could ever contain our great, loving God. So even if an ocean filled with ink were to be drained until it was dry, we would just have begun writing about "the love of God above."

Heavenly Father, thank You for choosing to love me. I feel secure, knowing that You'll never take Your love away. How I praise You for that!

bfs

He's Got the Whole World in His Hands

He's got the whole wide world in His hands.
He's got the whole wide world in His hands.
He's got the whole wide world in His hands.
He's got the whole world in His hands.

He's got the sun and the moon in His hands.
He's got the sun and the moon in His hands.
He's got the sun and the moon in His hands.
He's got the whole world in His hands.

He's got the sinner man in His hands.
He's got the sinner man in His hands.
He's got the whole wicked world in His hands.
He's got the whole world in His hands.

He's got the tiny little baby in His hands.
He's got the tiny little baby in His hands.
He's got that wee tiny little baby in His hands.
He's got the whole world in His hands.

He's got you and me, brother, in His hands.
He's got you and me, brother, in His hands.
He's got you and me, brother, in His hands;
He's got the whole world in His hands.

Traditional Spiritual

One of the most well-loved spirituals is "He's Got the Whole World in His Hands." I always enjoyed listening to the interpretation my favorite concert singer of a bygone era gave to this song. That was the American baritone John Charles Thomas. Mr. Thomas was featured on the *Coca-Cola Hour* on NBC radio for several years, later becoming a member of the Metropolitan Opera Company. It is of interest to note that the beloved Albert Hay Malotte's composition "The Lord's Prayer" was dedicated to his friend John Charles Thomas.

I had the privilege of meeting Mr. Thomas while he visited his mother in a Baltimore suburb. What a delight to tell him how much we enjoyed his singing. I mentioned a great favorite, "He's Got the Whole World in His Hands," and our fondness for his warm interpretation, particularly when he sang the words about the "tiny little baby." He asked me to go to the piano and accompany him, and he graciously helped me to give a warmer interpretation of this precious song.

In 1954, Mr. Graham was conducting a crusade in London. A gentleman there was telling us that he and his wife wanted to bring a neighbor to the meetings. The neighbor told this sweet couple he wanted nothing to do with "that business," but to please them, he finally came to one of the services. However, he seemed very uncomfortable and spoke out loud to those around him about his disapproval of what he was hearing.

In conversation later, we learned that it was part of this

song that touched this man's heart. Apparently, when I came to the verse about "the tiny little baby," the man slumped in his seat, overcome with emotion, for he had a very ill toddler at home. We also learned that when Mr. Graham spoke, this man listened intently to the message. When the tender invitation was given to bring your burdens to the Lord Jesus, he was one of the first to walk forward, giving his life to the Savior.

Come unto Me, all ye that labor and are heavy laden, and I will give you rest. Matthew 11:28, kjv

DEVOTIONAL INTERLUDE

Being in God's Hands

I HAVE ENGRAVED YOU ON THE PALMS OF MY HANDS.

ISAIAH 49:16, NIV

The spiritual says that God has "the *whole world* in His hands." Scripture reminds us that God also loves each one of us individually. According to Isaiah, each of us is engraved inside God's hands, where our image will never fade.

Then there's the "tiny little baby." Scripture tells us that when the little children ran out to meet Jesus, He lifted them into His arms and said, "Permit the children to come to Me, do not hinder them; for the kingdom of God belongs to such as these" (Mark 10:14, NASB).

As much as that father at the London meetings in 1954 cared about his tiny child, his love could not compare to God's love for every child.

> *Father, how great Your love is for all of Your children.*
> *I'm thankful to be able to leave my life in Your hands, for*
> *I know I can rest securely in Your loving care.*

bfs

Pass Me Not, O Gentle Savior

Pass me not, O gentle Savior,
Hear my humble cry;
While on others Thou art calling,
Do not pass me by.

Savior, Savior,
Hear my humble cry;
While on others Thou art calling,
Do not pass me by.

Let me at Thy throne of mercy
Find a sweet relief,
Kneeling there in deep contrition;
Help my unbelief.

Trusting only in Thy merit,
Would I seek Thy face;
Heal my wounded, broken spirit,
Save me by Thy grace.

Thou the Spring of all my comfort,
More than life to me,
Whom have I on earth beside Thee?
Whom in heav'n but Thee?

Words: Fanny J. Crosby (1820–1915)
Music: William H. Doane (1832–1915)

Pass Me Not, O Gentle Savior

In 1955 after the London crusade, Billy Graham and the team were asked to visit several American military bases in France and Germany. Our driver, a colonel, told us we were about to take a detour to Martin Luther's grave in the city of Rheims. Arriving about an hour before sunset, we noticed a group of men and women dressed in their Sunday best, the men wearing black suits with white shirts and ties. We saw they were looking at us intently. One of them pointed a finger and with a big broad smile said, quite loudly, "Billy GRAW-hum." Each man drew from his vest pocket a little hymnbook, and they sang to us. I saw Ruth Graham's eyes well with tears as she was filled with emotion at this sight. We all said "thank you," and Billy said to me, "Sing that song you did for the group of people who had just come over from East Berlin."

As best I could in the German language, I sang the tender words, "Pass me not, O gentle Savior. Hear my humble cry/While on others thou art calling, do not pass me by . . ." A local policeman arrived on the scene, appearing rather gruff. He looked around but then continued walking down the street. Then a fine-looking gentleman came along and greeted us in English. We asked him to interpret for us, and this made it possible for Mr. Graham to give a message of encouragement to this wonderful group of believers. We were told that they were from the Christian Railroad Association, enjoying an annual holiday.

I learned this song in German for the open-air meeting held at the Brandenburg Gate dividing East and West

Berlin. Some fifty thousand people came to hear Mr. Graham, speaking through his interpreter, Mr. Peter Schneider. It was said that twenty thousand crossed the line from East Berlin. The country was divided, but the Berlin Wall had not yet been built. It was still possible to cross from East to West. What a privilege to be there and to hear their singing. Mr. Graham was truly anointed of God as he spoke from the open Bible. When the invitation was tenderly extended, we were amazed at the number inquiring about faith in the Lord Jesus. They were asked to write their names and phone numbers in the space provided in the program so they could receive further encouragement on their spiritual journey.

There was one young nurse from East Berlin who came with her friends. She was quite skeptical at first but upon hearing the message, found herself wanting to accept Jesus as her Lord and Savior. She didn't have a pen or pencil, so she used her lipstick to write her name on the response portion of the program. In the crusade office the next day a counselor, looking at the huge number of filled-out cards, picked up one of them to find a name and phone number written clearly in very bright lipstick. How exciting to discover that the young lady had joyously come to faith in Christ. "Pass me not, O gentle Savior" is the heart cry of the song. Jesus had not passed her by! And He gave new life to the hundreds of others who called upon Him that memorable evening in West Berlin.

Some time later, Mr. Graham's interpreter, the young Peter Schneider, was introduced to this young lady. They fell in love and eventually married. God does indeed work in wonderful and mysterious ways.

DEVOTIONAL INTERLUDE

My Gentle Savior

ABRAHAM LOOKED UP AND SAW THREE MEN STANDING
NEARBY. WHEN HE SAW THEM, HE HURRIED FROM THE
ENTRANCE OF HIS TENT TO MEET THEM AND BOWED LOW TO
THE GROUND. HE SAID, "IF I HAVE FOUND FAVOR IN YOUR
EYES, MY LORD, DO NOT PASS YOUR SERVANT BY."

GENESIS 18:2-3, NIV

This hymn became very popular at the Moody-Sankey evangelistic services in London. It is based on a prayer that
Fanny Crosby heard someone pray—the same prayer that
Abraham prayed when he saw three visitors coming. Abraham understood that one of those men was the Lord, and he
didn't intend to miss out on that special visit.

We know that our Savior would never pass by anyone
who calls out to Him. He didn't pass by Bartimaeus or the
lepers or the children whose parents brought them to Him.
And He won't pass us by when He hears our "humble cry."
As we reach out to Jesus, He and His representatives—our
Christian friends—are all around us, supporting and
encouraging us.

> *Thank You, Lord Jesus, for never even considering the*
> *thought of passing me by. I love You, Lord, and trust You*
> *to meet my every need.*

bfs

How Big Is God

How big is God!
How big and wide His vast domain;
To try to tell, these lips can only start.
He's big enough
To rule His mighty universe,
Yet small enough to live within the heart.

'Though man may strive
To go beyond the reef of space,
To crawl beyond the distant glimm'ring stars,
The world's a room so small
Within my Master's house,
The open sky but a portion of His yard.

As winter's chill
May cause the tiny seed to fall,
To lie asleep till waked by summer rain.
The heart grown cold
Will warm and throb with life anew.
The Master's touch will bring the glow again.

Words and Music: Stuart Hamblen (1908–1989)
Copyright © 1959, renewed 1987 by Hamblen Music Company, P.O. Box 1937, Canyon Country, CA 91386. All rights reserved. International copyright secured. Used by permission. (ASCAP)

*S*tuart Hamblen wrote "How Big Is God," along with other great songs, such as "It Is No Secret," "This Old House," and many more favorites. He was a special friend of all of us on the Billy Graham team. We met him at the 1949 meetings in Los Angeles and many times thereafter.

Before he began writing gospel music, Stuart was famous for his western songs. Growing up in Texas, he went into radio broadcasting and became known as a singing cowboy. As a young man, he moved to Hollywood and for several years had a much-listened-to program on Warner Brothers radio in the late afternoon, Monday through Friday.

Stuart was a preacher's son, but he had wandered away from the Lord. He was on the air for about twenty years before renewing his faith in Christ. In 1949, Mr. Graham and all of the team were in Los Angeles for evangelistic meetings being held under what was called "The Big Tent." We were on a prayer-time radio program just ahead of Stuart Hamblen's show.

Stuart's wife, Suzie, was very involved in our meetings. She knew he would be sympathetic to us and invite us to his radio show. He told everyone to attend Mr. Graham's meetings and said he was planning to attend, which he did.

We were all praying for Stuart. One time when I went back to Chicago to do my regular *Club Time* radio program on ABC radio, I missed a Tuesday night meeting. I heard afterward that Stuart Hamblen had found the Lord. He was unable to sleep that night. Around 4:00 A.M. he called the hotel and requested to see Mr. Graham. When Stuart arrived at 5:00 A.M., Billy Graham, T.W. Wilson, and Grady Wilson prayed with him, as Stuart returned to faith in Christ as his Savior. This was a time of great rejoicing.

"Oh, I must call Mama," Stuart said. As he talked to her, he told Mr. Graham, "She's crying." We know, of course, that those were tears of joy.

After this wonderful experience, Stuart soon entered a new popular venture, *The Cowboy Church of the Air,* which was syndicated nationwide. However, because he refused to air a commercial for an alcoholic product, his sponsors dropped the show.

Stuart began writing gospel songs and was very successful at it. One was titled "How Big Is God." I felt so honored when I learned that he wrote that song especially for me. I have his original pencil manuscript. Songwriter Bill Gaither once said to me, "Take care of that one!"

About ten days before Stuart Hamblen went to be with the Lord, I talked to him in the hospital. I said, "I have the original in my hand, Stuart—the music you composed for me. You wrote at the top of the song, 'I love you, Bev.'" Stuart responded, "I wrote that because I do."

That meant a lot to me.

Stuart also wrote another song I love to sing and like to recall often:

But until then my heart will go on singing,
Until then with joy I'll carry on,
Until the day my eyes behold the city,
Until the day God calls me home.

Discovering How Big God Is

GOD PROMISED EVERYTHING TO THE SON AS AN INHERI-
TANCE, AND THROUGH THE SON HE MADE THE UNIVERSE
AND EVERYTHING IN IT. THE SON REFLECTS GOD'S OWN
GLORY, AND EVERYTHING ABOUT HIM REPRESENTS GOD
EXACTLY. HE SUSTAINS THE UNIVERSE BY THE MIGHTY
POWER OF HIS COMMAND.   HEBREWS 1:2-3, NLT

Some have traveled into space and announced that they
didn't find God out there. How small their god is—they
have seen "a portion of His yard," but they haven't recognized God's handiwork.

As God's children, it's our privilege to have God's Holy
Spirit living in our hearts (Galatians 4:6). God's Spirit
enables us to understand who He really is.

A powerful Creator could have gone away and left His
work of creation to fend for itself. But a loving God
couldn't do that. Just as He sends the warm rain to awaken
tiny seeds, so He sends His warm touch to bring our cold
hearts to life. What a big, loving God He is!

> *Creator and Ruler of the universe, I see the stars, the*
> *moon, and the sun, and I realize how big You are. But*
> *what thrills me most of all is the warmth of Your loving*
> *presence in my heart.*

bfs

How Long Has It Been?

How long has it been since you talked with the
  Lord
And told Him your heart's hidden secrets?
How long since you prayed,
How long since you stayed
On your knees 'til the light shone through?

How long has it been since your mind felt at ease?
How long since your heart knew no burden?
Can you call Him your friend?
How long has it been
Since you knew that He cared for you?

How long has it been since you knelt by your bed
And prayed to the Lord up in heaven?
How long since you knew
That He'd answer you,
And would keep you the long night through?

How long has it been since you woke with the
  dawn
And felt that the day's worth the living?
Can you call Him your friend?
How long has it been
Since you knew that He cared for you?

Words and Music: Mosie Lister (b. 1921)
Copyright © 1956 Mosie Lister Songs.
(Administered by The Copyright Co., Nashville, TN) Renewed 1991.

How Long Has It Been?

*A*fter having been a widower for many years, I was thankful for the opportnity to marry Karlene in 1985. (You can read more about that on pages 215–217.)

Karlene and I have developed many wonderful friendships over the years. We have precious friends in Kentucky whose main goal in life is winning people to the Lord. They have a lovely home, which they enjoy sharing with other people—entertaining dinner guests often.

Some time ago they invited the Barrows and the Sheas to spend a weekend with them. We had such a good time together.

As we took a few minutes to relax in our room, our hostess slipped a paper under the door with a list of the guests for the evening. To us, it looked as if she had invited practically the whole town, including the mayor!

After dinner, our hostess said to Cliff and me, "Maybe you can sing something." Because it was such a diverse crowd, she couldn't just say that she was going to have us sing hymns; but, of course, she was hoping we would.

As Cliff's wife, Billie, went to the piano, a lady way in the back of the huge living room said, "Do you know 'How Long Has It Been?' " That warmed my heart. I thought, *Wouldn't that be something to sing that song here this evening?*

I asked Billie if she knew the melody. "What key?" she asked. "E-flat," I replied. So we began, "How long has it been since you talked with the Lord and told Him your heart's hidden secrets?"

When the song was finished, the person who had made

the request was weeping. Soon this diverse audience was asking only for wonderful old hymns and gospel songs.

It was indeed a precious time, just what our gracious hosts had prayed for. And it was a joy for me to sing these hymn-songs, so dear to our hearts. We prayed that lives would be touched.

Thank you, Lord!

DEVOTIONAL INTERLUDE

Talking with the Lord

MY HEART HAS HEARD YOU SAY, "COME AND TALK WITH ME." AND MY HEART RESPONDS, "LORD, I AM COMING."

PSALM 27:8, NLT

CAST ALL YOUR ANXIETY ON HIM BECAUSE HE CARES FOR YOU.   1 PETER 5:7, NIV

If we're unable to communicate regularly with friends, we lose touch with each other's lives. Eventually, the friendship is no longer as close as it once was.

Our friendship with God is like that. He looks forward to having us share our most intimate secrets regularly with Him. He doesn't want us to forget that He is there and desires to share our burdens.

Nighttime seems to be when problems—big and small—most often overwhelm us. Isn't it wonderful that we have a heavenly Father who invites us to come and talk with Him at any time of the day or night?

Thank You, Father, for listening whenever I talk with You, and for assuring me of Your care. May there never be a long time between our visits.

bfs

I Found a Friend

I found a Friend when life seemed not worth living.
I found a Friend so tender and forgiving.
I can't conceive how such a thing could be,
That Jesus cares for even me.
Each day, each year, my faith in Him is growing.
He's ever near, His love is overflowing.
I have no fear, my worldly cares are few.
I can depend on Him to see me through.
I found a Friend, He can be your Friend too.

I found a Friend and now He walks beside me.
His hand to lend to comfort and to guide me,
When clouds appear I talk with Him awhile,
He's taught this heart of mine to smile.
Because He came my soul will live in glory.
I'll praise His name and tell my Saviour's story.
What friend so true would give his all for you?
I found a Friend and life began anew.
I'm sure you'll find that He is your friend too.

Words: Roc Hillman (b. 1911)
Music: Barclay Allen (1918–1966)
Copyright © 1953 by Merit Music Co., Hollywood, CA; Cinephonic Music
Co. Ltd. 17 Berners St., London. Copyright renewed 1981. International copyright secured.

*A*musical number that I sometimes sing just before Mr. Graham speaks is titled "I Found a Friend," written by Barclay Allen and Roc Hillman in 1953.

One memorable evening included this song before Mr. Graham's message at a stadium in Boise, Idaho. Making his way to the pulpit, Mr. Graham turned to me and said, "When you sang 'I Found a Friend' tonight, you had no idea that the son of the composer was seated beside me."

I turned and saw Dr. Ronald Allen, a theology professor from the West Coast, with a large smile on his face. After the meeting we greeted each other so warmly and had a wonderful time talking together.

Ronald's father, Barclay Allen, was a pianist with Freddy Martin's popular band in the 1940s. He traveled with the band, made recordings, and performed for some time at a large hotel in Los Angeles.

In 1948, Mr. Allen started his own band and went on an eighteen-month road trip to Denver, St. Louis, Memphis, Chicago, then back west to Boise, San Francisco, and Lake Tahoe.

Barclay Allen did not know our Lord as his Savior in those years. One night while driving alone to Reno, he fell asleep at the wheel, missed a turn on a mountain highway, and crashed his car. Suffering from a broken neck, he was told that he would never walk nor play the piano again. This thirty-year-old successful musician became very discouraged and almost angry with God.

A pastor, the Rev. Norman Hammer, began visiting Barclay. At first Barclay wanted nothing to do with him. But the pastor kept coming and finally led the young pianist to the Lord. Barclay slowly regained strength and was able to use his arms and hands to play the piano again.

Mr. Allen's friend Roc Hillman wanted to create a song that would tell this wonderful conversion story and would also speak to a broad audience.

Using Barclay's music, Mr. Hillman wrote the words for "I Found a Friend."[4]

---

[4]Editor's note: Much of the information contained in the story above is based on material from the book *Lord of Song* (Multnomah Press, 1985) by Barclay Allen's son, Ronald.

Depending on My Friend

AS THE FATHER HAS LOVED ME, SO HAVE I LOVED YOU. NOW REMAIN IN MY LOVE. . . . GREATER LOVE HAS NO ONE THAN THIS, THAT ONE LAY DOWN HIS LIFE FOR HIS FRIENDS.

JOHN 15:9, 13, NIV

The love of God the Father for God the Son illustrates the Son's love for each of us. Jesus came to earth to show what a special Friend He is—a Friend everyone can find.

Jesus tells us that God the Father loved Him and gave Him glory "even before the world began" (John 17:24, NLT). The Son, who has always existed with the Father, doesn't set Himself apart from us. Shortly before His crucifixion, He prayed, telling His Father in heaven that He wanted His friends to be with Him and see His glory someday.

Isn't it wonderful to know that our Friend and Savior, who gives us life "anew," is with us, walking constantly beside us? We can talk to Him, and receive comfort and guidance from Him, no matter how big the clouds around us seem to be.

Lord Jesus, I'm so glad that I found You. I know I can depend on You in all circumstances. Thank You for being a true Savior and Friend—for giving Your life so I can have new life with You and someday "live in glory."

bfs

If We Could See Beyond Today

If we could see beyond today
As God can see,
If all the clouds should roll away,
The shadows flee;
O'er present griefs we would not fret,
Each sorrow we would soon forget,
For many joys are waiting yet,
For you and me.

If we could know beyond today
As God doth know,
Why dearest treasures pass away
And tears must flow;
And why the darkness leads to light,
Why dreary days will soon grow bright:
Someday life's wrongs will be made right—
Faith tells us so.

If we could see, if we could know—
We often say,
But God in love a veil doth throw
Across our way;
We cannot see what lies before,
And so we cling to Him the more:
He leads us till this life is o'er.
Trust and obey.

Words: Unknown
Music: Norman J. Clayton (1903–1978)
Music copyright © 1943 Wordspring Music, Inc. Renewed 1971, Norman
Clayton Publishing Co., owner. International copyright secured. All rights
reserved. Used by permission. Author of lyrics is unknown.

If We Could See Beyond Today

We seem to think that unexplained, violent loss of life happens only to other people. But a terrible tragedy struck—an intruder broke into the home of a neighbor's beloved sister and took the life of one of our dear friends.

When we received the call, I was at home between travels. We attended the graveside service. As family and friends stood there in unbelievable grief, the pastor beckoned to me, saying quietly, "Please sing something appropriate." My heart jumped, and I wondered to myself, *What can I do? What song could be appropriate?* Karlene took my arm and gave loving support as it came to me that I should sing only the middle verse of the comforting old song "If We Could See Beyond Today":

If we could know beyond today
As God doth know,
Why dearest treasures pass away
And tears must flow;
And why the darkness leads to light,
Why dreary paths will soon grow bright,
Someday life's wrongs will be made right—
Faith tells us so.

Finishing that verse, I bowed out and stepped back into the group gathered there. I felt so grateful that these precious words had been brought back to mind and could be used to comfort family members and friends.

Some who were there said that this song was the only thing that helped them get through the day. We were all still dealing with the shock and pain of a dreadful event. We could see it only from a finite point of view and could not find a reason why it had happened!

The young man who had committed this horrendous crime was only seventeen years old. The police identified and located him. He was armed at the time of his arrest and was later convicted.

The young woman whose life was taken and her sister were both graduates of Wheaton College in Wheaton, Illinois, and had been living victorious Christian lives in every way. Yes, we want to know why this happened. But today we can see that the young woman's sister has developed a ministry with people who have experienced tragedies such as this in their families. Out of one evil act, God has brought hope and help to others.

While it is natural to ask why, we do know that "Someday life's wrongs will be made right. Faith tells us so."

And the faith we speak of is our shelter in the critical hour.

DEVOTIONAL INTERLUDE

All That's Beyond

THOUGH YOU HAVE MADE ME SEE TROUBLES, MANY AND
BITTER, YOU WILL RESTORE MY LIFE AGAIN; FROM THE
DEPTHS OF THE EARTH YOU WILL AGAIN BRING ME UP.

PSALM 71:20, NIV

Parents try to protect their children from the worries of
adulthood. God also desires to protect His children. One
way He does this is by permitting us to see nothing more
than the present moment.

God is a Father who understands all things from an eternal perspective. He knows that He will be with us to see us
through all that we will face in the future, and He wants us
to have the faith to believe He will do this. We can be confident that God sees far beyond this day or the next, and His
faithfulness to us will never end.

We might wish that we could immediately make right
all the wrongs we see. That's for God to do   and He will.

> *Dear God, sometimes it seems impossible to understand
> "our present griefs," but we know You are a loving God
> who will care for us through them all. Thank You,
> Father, for wiping our tears away. Give us the faith we
> need to trust all of our future days to You.*

bfs

In the Garden

I come to the garden alone,
While the dew is still on the roses;
And the voice I hear, falling on my ear,
The Son of God discloses.

And He walks with me, and He talks with me,
And He tells me I am His own;
And the joy we share as we tarry there,
None other has ever known.

He speaks, and the sound of His voice
Is so sweet the birds hush their singing;
And the melody that He gave to me
Within my heart is ringing.

I'd stay in the garden with Him
Tho' the night around me be falling;
But He bids me go; thro' the voice of woe,
His voice to me is calling.

Words and Music: C. Austin Miles (1868–1946)
Copyright © 1912 by Hall-Mack Co. Renewed 1940 (extended).
The Rodeheaver Co., owner. Copyright © 1964 by The Rodeheaver Co.
International copyright secured. All rights reserved. Used by permission.

I remember singing this beautiful song at Madison Square Garden in New York for the Billy Graham Crusade in 1957. On that first night I chose a song I thought surely was a favorite of many. At the time, I was innocent of the irony, but with twenty thousand people filling Madison Square Garden, I stepped to the podium and began, "I come to the garden *alone.*" I thought there were some smiles from the crowd! Cliff and Billy teased me about the choice of that song for several weeks. Every now and then we bring it up again.

Composer Charles Austin Miles changed careers when he was in his midtwenties. He first studied to be a pharmacist but soon abandoned that profession to become a songwriter. It was through this gift that he felt most useful to his Master.

Miles wrote a detailed account of how he received the inspiration to write "In the Garden," while reading John 20 in April of 1912. He was sitting in his darkroom, where, in addition to photographic equipment, he had a beloved Estey reed organ.

As Mr. Miles read the story of how Mary met Jesus shortly after the Resurrection, it was as if Miles became part of the scene. He saw Mary, dressed in white, her head bowed, walking down a winding path shaded by olive branches. In his mind's eye, he saw her as she looked inside the tomb and began to weep. Then she turned and saw Jesus. Miles wrote that he, too, saw the figure behind Mary in the scene and knew it was the Lord Jesus.

Mr. Miles immediately began to write the words exactly as we now sing them. That same evening there came to him the touching music that blends so well with the poetic message.

Walking and Talking with Our Lord

MARY . . . SAW SOMEONE STANDING BEHIND HER. IT WAS JESUS, BUT SHE DIDN'T RECOGNIZE HIM. . . . "SIR," SHE SAID, "IF YOU HAVE TAKEN HIM AWAY, TELL ME WHERE YOU HAVE PUT HIM, AND I WILL GO AND GET HIM." "MARY!" JESUS SAID. SHE TURNED TOWARD HIM AND EXCLAIMED, "TEACHER!" JOHN 20:11-16, NLT

At the beginning of time, Adam and Eve "heard the sound of the Lord God as he was walking in the garden in the cool of the day" (Genesis 3:8, NLT). But because they knew they had disobeyed God, they hid from Him.

When our Lord Jesus came to earth, died, and rose again, he took the blame for all of our sin. Now He walks with *us;* and just like Mary in the garden by the tomb, we hear Him. He tells us we are "His own"—what a joy "as we tarry there."

Thank You, Jesus, for coming to be my Savior and Lord.
Thank You for walking and talking with me, and for tell-
ing me that I am Your own. You bring a melody to my
heart that will remain forever.

bfs

Because He Lives

God sent His Son, they called Him Jesus,
He came to love, heal, and forgive;
He lived and died to buy my pardon,
An empty grave is there to prove my Savior lives.

Because He lives I can face tomorrow,
Because He lives all fear is gone;
Because I know He holds the future.
And life is worth the living just because He lives.

How sweet to hold a newborn baby,
And feel the pride and joy he gives;
But greater still the calm assurance,
This child can face uncertain days because He lives.

And then one day I'll cross the river,
I'll fight life's final war with pain;
And then as death gives way to victory,
I'll see the lights of glory and I'll know He lives.

Words: William J. Gaither and Gloria Gaither
Music: William J. Gaither
Copyright © 1971, 1980 by William J. Gaither, Inc. All rights reserved.
Used by permission of Gaither Copyright Management.

I have had the privilege of meeting so many wonderful people over the years. One young man I've enjoyed coming to know is Michael Tait of the Christian group dc Talk.

I remember when Michael came to our home. He talked about his father, a retired pastor, and I mentioned that we are both "preacher's kids." He spoke warmly of his happy home life as he was growing up. While Michael was at our house, his father reached another milestone. Michael pulled a cell phone from his pocket, and soon we were singing "Happy Birthday" across the miles.

Eddie De Garmo, of Forefront Records, asked me to come to Nashville to record Bill Gaither's "Because He Lives" as a duet with Michael. Mr. De Garmo met me at the Nashville airport and we drove to the nearby city of Brentwood, arriving at the studio where the young men of dc Talk do most of their recording.

They placed me at a small table where a microphone and headphones were set up. Soon I was hearing a large prerecorded orchestra begin the introduction to "Because He Lives." As instructed, I began to sing "God sent His Son, they called Him Jesus/He came to love, heal, and forgive." Coming to the end of the verse I heard some powerful drums, carrying over into the chorus, which was to be sung by Michael Tait in his beautiful tenor voice. I removed the headphones as Michael came into the studio to do the continuing voice-over. Director Eddie De Garmo delayed further recording for a few minutes so that Michael and I could take a break and renew our friendship. We had a great time talking, and some of our conversation found its way onto the recording. When Michael sang his part, his tenor voice on the chorus was marvelous.

It is so wonderful that music, which is often cited for dividing generations, can and many times does bring them together.

DEVOTIONAL INTERLUDE
A Life Worth Living

[JESUS SAID,] "BEFORE LONG, THE WORLD WILL NOT SEE ME ANYMORE, BUT YOU WILL SEE ME. BECAUSE I LIVE, YOU ALSO WILL LIVE." JOHN 14:19, NIV

Bill and Gloria Gaither were expecting their third child in the late 1960s. They had been going through some discouraging times, and Bill was exhausted from a bout with mononucleosis. It was an unsettling time in society because of drugs, racial tensions, and the belief by many that God was dead.

Gloria began wondering what their new baby would be facing. But as she sat in her living room, she felt Jesus' presence reassuring her that because of the Resurrection, He was victorious. She and Bill could trust God to bring joy and peace to their future. And so they wrote the song that reminds us that we, too, "can face uncertain days."

From the time when we come into this life as "a newborn baby" to the time when we "cross the river" into heaven, our very-much-alive Savior is by our side, revealing God's love and making life "worth the living."

> *Dear God, You have shown me how great Your love is by sending Your Son to be my victorious, ever-present, loving, living Savior. How I praise You for giving me a life that's worth living!*

bfs

It Is No Secret

The chimes of time ring out the news:
Another day is through.
Someone slipped and fell.
Was that someone you?
You may have longed for added strength,
Your courage to renew.
Do not be disheartened,
For I bring hope to you.

It is no secret
What God can do.
What He's done for others,
He'll do for you.
With arms wide open,
He'll pardon you.
It is no secret
What God can do.

There is no night, for in His light
You'll never walk alone.
Always feel at home
Wherever you may roam.
There is no power can conquer you,
While God is on your side.
Just take Him at His promise;
Don't run away and hide.

Words and Music: Stuart Hamblen (1908–1989)
Copyright © 1950 Songs of Universal, Inc.
(Administered by Universal MCA Music Publishing)

It Is No Secret

*O*ur friend Stuart Hamblen once said, "I try to write music with a spiritual uplift instead of a moral downbeat." Perhaps that's what has made Stuart's music so popular and loved by so many.

It is no secret that this song is Stuart Hamblen's most well-known and best-loved composition. Now considered a classic, it was one of the first religious songs to "cross over," as the expression goes, and become popular in both the religious and mainstream markets. "It Is No Secret" has been translated into more than fifty languages!

Ralph Carmichael, one of the pioneers of contemporary Christian music, has said that Stuart Hamblen was way ahead of his time, reaching and ministering through his music not only to Christians, but also to others long before the rest of us ever thought that would be possible. He was able to do this because of the marvelous content of his poetry, so descriptive of the needs and emotions of the human heart.

Mr. Hamblen heard that "It Is No Secret" was not being played on BBC Radio in England. Flying to London, he met with the broadcasters and said, "This song is being heard all over the U.S.A. and Canada. I would be so happy if you could play it here." They stated, "We *cannot* air this song because it mentions God." Stuart, in true Texas cowboy style, responded, "Ah, gentlemen, you're not telling me you have stopped singing the national anthem, 'God Save the Queen'!"

Consequently, this song also became a great favorite in

the United Kingdom, Europe, Australia, and New Zealand. Through an open Amsterdam hotel window at 6:30 in the morning I heard a gentleman out on the street whistling "It Is No Secret." Chuckling, I hastily wrote Stuart a postcard describing the incident.

The origin of this song dates back to 1949. Not long after coming to faith at the Billy Graham meetings in Los Angeles, Stuart met John Wayne while walking down Hollywood Boulevard. They had become good friends while working on films together and John said, "I've been reading in the paper about what happened to you, Stuart."

Stuart replied, "Well, it's no secret what God can do."

John's response: "That sounds like a song to me."

Stuart went home encouraged by the thought. Just as the clock was chiming midnight, Stuart sat down at his Hammond organ and began writing, "The chimes of time ring out the news: another day is through. . . . It is no secret what God can do. What He's done for others, He'll do for you."

What a song, written at the midnight hour!

DEVOTIONAL INTERLUDE

What God Can Do

GOD'S SECRET PLAN HAS NOW BEEN REVEALED TO US; IT IS A
PLAN CENTERED ON CHRIST, DESIGNED LONG AGO ACCORD-
ING TO HIS GOOD PLEASURE.   EPHESIANS 1:9, NLT

A chiming clock can be a pleasant sound, lulling us to sleep.
But slumber is often delayed as thoughts float back and
forth: *Did I encourage anyone today? Did I ask the Lord to
help me serve Him?*

 The Lord Jesus provides the strength and courage each
step of the way. We need not "run away and hide," for God
is with us.

> *Father, I don't want to slip and fall from the path we've
> been walking on together. But if I do, remind me to hurry
> back into Your wide-open arms. When I'm feeling lonely
> or in the dark, remind me that Your Son, Jesus, is my
> Light, and He will never leave me. Thank You, God, for
> being my loving and forgiving Father. "It is no secret"
> what You have done for me.*

bfs

Ivory Palaces

My Lord has garments so wondrous fine,
And myrrh their texture fills;
Its fragrance reached to this heart of mine,
With joy my being thrills.

Out of the ivory palaces,
Into a world of woe,
Only His great, eternal love
Made my Savior go.

His life had also its sorrows sore,
For aloes had a part;
And when I think of the cross He bore,
My eyes with teardrops start.

His garments too were in cassia dipped,
With healing in a touch;
Each time my feet in some sin have slipped,
He took me from its clutch.

In garments glorious He will come,
To open wide the door;
And I shall enter my heavenly home,
To dwell forevermore.

Words and Music: Henry Barraclough (1891–1983)

Ivory Palaces

*I*t was in the area of Montreat and Black Mountain, North Carolina, in 1915 that Henry Barraclough wrote the words and music to the beautiful hymn "Ivory Palaces." The idea for the hymn came from a sermon by Dr. J. Wilbur Chapman on Psalm 45:8. Here Christ is pictured as coming out of the ivory palaces of heaven to redeem humankind, clothed in fine garments, perfumed with myrrh for beauty, aloes for bitterness, and cassia for healing—the fragrance which is a reminder of His near presence.

Henry Barraclough was born in England, where he studied organ and piano from the age of five, later coming to America as a young man.

What a privilege it was for us to meet Mr. Barraclough after enjoying his hymn for so many years. He was with us at Mr. Graham's Philadelphia crusade one year, appointed as the local treasurer. He was then sixty-five years of age. Of course, we sang this hymn at the meetings for the spiritual uplift it gave to all of us.

What a joy, what a privilege to lift our voices to sing "Ivory Palaces." It's wonderful to experience the beautiful fragrance of redemption in the presence of our God as we worship Him.

Dwelling in My Lord's Palaces

GOD, YOUR GOD, HAS ANOINTED YOU, POURING OUT THE OIL OF JOY ON YOU MORE THAN ON ANYONE ELSE. YOUR ROBES ARE PERFUMED WITH MYRRH, ALOES, AND CASSIA. IN PALACES DECORATED WITH IVORY, YOU ARE ENTERTAINED BY THE MUSIC OF HARPS.   PSALM 45:7-8, NLT

Psalm 45, which describes a special king who wears perfumed robes and lives in ivory palaces, is a messianic psalm. It's in Hebrews 1:6 that this king is identified as God's Son.

Why would our Savior leave "palaces of ivory" to come to a place filled with sin and sadness? The answer, of course, is that nothing other than "His great eternal love" could have made Him willing to give up His home.

Love made God the Son willing to leave heaven and bear the cross so that someday He can "open wide the door" to heaven for us. Love makes us willing to give control of our life to Him so that we'll be ready to enter our heavenly home with Jesus, the Lamb of God.

My Savior and Lord, my eyes fill with tears of joy and thanksgiving when I think about the "ivory palaces" You left for me. Now I wait for the day when the door to heaven will open wide so I can "dwell forevermore" with the King of Heaven!

bfs

Little Is Much When God Is in It

In the harvest field now ripened,
There's a work for all to do;
Hark! The voice of God is calling,
To the harvest calling you.

Little is much when God is in it,
Labor not for wealth or fame;
There's a crown and you can win it,
If you'll go in Jesus' name.

Does the place you're called to labor
Seem so small and little known?
It is great if God is in it,
And He'll not forget His own.

Are you laid aside from service,
Body worn from toil and care?
You can still be in the battle,
In the sacred place of pray'r.

Words: Kittie J. Suffield (1884–1972)
Music: Dwight Brock (b. 1907)
Copyright © 1969 Stamps-Baxter Music (Administered by Brentwood-Benson
Music Publishing, 741 Cool Springs Blvd., Franklin TN 37067)

Fred Suffield came to faith in Christ during special
services in my father's church in Winchester, Ontario. He
seemed to naturally develop the gift of speaking. Dad and
others observed how he so effectively witnessed about his
newfound faith in Jesus.

Fred, a successful Winchester farmer, began to feel the
call of God on his life to become a preacher of the gospel.
One day while standing in a hayfield next to the Canadian
Pacific Railroad tracks, Fred looked up into the heavens as
he drove his pitchfork into the ground. Then he exclaimed,
"All right, Lord, I will be your witness behind the pulpit
anywhere, if that is what you want me to be!" Leaving the
pitchfork there, he never looked back. He sought my
father's counsel and together they prayed that God would
give Fred real peace and direction.

What happened next is a wonderful story of God bringing a man and woman together to do His work.

My father held a week of meetings at his Wesleyan
Church. Kittie, a singer from the U.S., was invited to be the
soloist for the evening services. During the week the winter's
snow came in an unusual fashion—several feet of it. When
it was time for Kittie to return to her home in New York
State, she boarded the Canadian Pacific train for the trip
south. Would you believe the beautiful, black steam locomotive became wedged in the tall snowdrifts? It came to a
halt three miles from the station and some two hundred
yards from the Suffield farm.

Fred quickly harnessed his big Clydesdale horses to his

farm sleigh, and making his way through the drifts, arrived at the tracks. He was able to bring several of the passengers to his home. Kittie was among them. They had to stay the night. All week the young Mr. Suffield had been enjoying the singing of this fine soprano/pianist, and now here she was, delivered right to his home with the other stranded passengers. After breakfast the next morning, when the time came to leave, their eyes met at the door. That was quite a beginning for a romance that lasted a lifetime.

Fred and Kittie asked if they could be married in our home. The wedding took place on a Saturday evening. We children were upstairs with our hands cupped to our ears, listening to everything that was happening. In a little while we heard them say good-bye as they rushed to the railway station for a train to Toronto.

Kittie wrote a number of songs, including "God Is Still on the Throne" and "Little Is Much When God Is in It." A fine singer, accomplished pianist, and songwriter, Kittie was always at Fred's side to assist him in his ministry.

I remember the day when Kittie excitedly showed me an envelope she had just received with a blue sheet of paper—the printed proof of her new song "Little Is Much When God Is in It." Through the years, it has been a fine selection to include in dedication services for Christian workers.

As a gospel singer, it has been my privilege to include this wonderful song in crusades around the globe.

Sir David McNee, retired Commissioner of Police of the Metropolis (London, U.K.) based at New Scotland Yard, came to love the song when he heard it in 1966 at the Earl's Court Billy Graham Crusade. Every time we would meet or talk on the phone after that, he would begin singing in his wonderful tenor voice, "Little is much when God is in it. . . ."

DEVOTIONAL INTERLUDE

The Little That Becomes Much

HERE IS A BOY WITH FIVE SMALL BARLEY LOAVES AND TWO
SMALL FISH, BUT HOW FAR WILL THEY GO AMONG SO MANY?

JOHN 6:9, NIV

How wonderful it will be someday if others are in heaven
because of our faithful witness! Sometimes we look at the
huge fields of souls ready to be harvested, and the job looks
too big. But the truth of the matter is that the majority of
God's work is done one-on-one, through friendship,
witnessing, and counseling.

The boy who gave his little lunch to Jesus had no idea
how much he really was giving. How surprised he must have
been to see what Jesus did with his lunch! But, knowing that
story, we need not be surprised that as a result of our Christian witness, little can be much—"when God is in it."

Dear Lord, thank You for taking the little that I have to
offer and turning it into much good for Your Kingdom.
I praise You for the privilege of serving You, no matter
where You choose to use me. May my labors always
be for Your glory.

bfs

Go Down, Moses

When Israel was in Egypt land—
Let my people go!
Oppressed so hard they could not stand—
Let my people go!

Go down, Moses,
Way down in Egypt land.
Tell old Pharaoh,
"Let my people go!"

"Thus saith the Lord," bold Moses said:
Let my people go!
"If not, I'll smite your firstborn dead."
Let my people go!

"No more shall they in bondage toil,"
Let my people go!
"Let them come out with Egypt's spoil,"
Let my people go!

Traditional Spiritual

*I*n my early twenties I was clerking in the medical department of Mutual Life Insurance in New York, located where the World Trade Center was built some thirty years later. While there I met some interesting personalities. Those that stand out in my memory include the then vigorous young baseball player Lou Gehrig, newsman Frank Gannett, and the NBC comedian Fred Allen.

Mr. Allen's insurance agent had brought him in for the routine exam given when applying for life insurance. Pointing to me he said, "This young fellow sings." He had heard that I was studying with the noted voice coach, Manley Price Boone.

Fred Allen asked if I'd like to audition for the part of his broadcast devoted to amateur performers. I went for the audition and was invited to be on the show, reporting to Studio 8-H. That famous studio is still used in New York.

The day before the broadcast, I went to a gentleman in Times Square who made 78 rpm records of on-air performances. I paid him $3.50 to make a small aluminum record that could be played with a wooden needle (or a thorn). He recorded my few minutes at the microphone. The record is still somewhere in my basement (called the "Sheasonian" by my wife, Karlene).

I was a little nervous about singing live in front of fifteen hundred people, plus the nationwide radio audience. Fred Allen said to me, "I understand you are from Canada. They play a lot of hockey up there. I have a new definition of hockey. I would like to try it out on you: Hockey is the same as polo, except on a horse and in winter" (Fred Allen was famous for saying things backwards). The audience chuckled, then Mr. Allen asked, "What's the name of your song?" I said, "Go Down, Moses." He replied, "Well, *go down, Moses!*"

I sang the song twice. The first broadcast was for the East Coast audience. Then we did the program again at midnight New York time for the West Coast audience—everything was "live" in the early days of radio. I thought the song went quite well, and I hit a strong low E bass note at the end of the song. The people seemed to like that. I was awarded second prize. First prize went to a yodeler. He was very good and deserving of the top accolade.

DEVOTIONAL INTERLUDE

God Lets His People Go

THE LORD SAID TO MOSES, "PHARAOH IS VERY STUBBORN, AND HE CONTINUES TO REFUSE TO LET THE PEOPLE GO. . . . SAY TO HIM, 'THE LORD, THE GOD OF THE HEBREWS, HAS SENT ME TO SAY, "LET MY PEOPLE GO, SO THEY CAN WORSHIP ME IN THE WILDERNESS.'" EXODUS 7:14-16, NLT

The story of Moses going down to Egypt to free the Hebrew slaves touched the African-American slaves of the nineteenth century. It became the theme of this song. These freedom songs often had messages that referred to both physical and spiritual bondage.

Today we may feel that we're held captive by an unhappy relationship; a job that brings no satisfaction; or, as Proverbs 5:22 explains, by sins that have us in their grip. The words of the spirituals fascinate us as we look for different types of liberation.

"Go Down, Moses" reminds us that just as God worked through Moses to release the Hebrew people from slavery, we, too, can be released. When we pray, God says, "Let my people go."

Lord, thank You for freedom from oppression and sin.
Thank You for spirituals that help me express my desire
for freedom and my joy as I experience it in You.

bfs

The King Is Coming

The marketplace is empty,
No more traffic in the streets.
All the builders' tools are silent,
No more time to harvest wheat;
Busy housewives cease their labors,
In the courtroom no debate,
Work on earth is all suspended
As the King comes through the gate!

O the King is coming,
The King is coming!
I just heard the trumpets sounding,
And now His face I see.
O the King is coming,
The King is coming!
Praise God, He's coming for me!

Happy faces line the hallways,
Those whose lives have been redeemed,
Broken homes that He has mended,
Those from prison He has freed;
Little children and the aged,
Hand in hand stand all aglow,
Who were crippled, broken, ruined,
Clad in garments white as snow.

I can hear the chariots rumble,
I can see the marching throng,
The flurry of God's trumpets
Spells the end of sin and wrong;
Regal robes are now unfolding,
Heaven's grandstands all in place,
Heaven's choir is now assembled,
Start to sing "Amazing Grace!"

Words: William J. Gaither and Gloria Gaither
Words, stanza 3: Written with Charles Millhuff
Music: William J. Gaither
Copyright © 1970 by William J. Gaither. All rights reserved. Used by permission of Gaither Copyright Management.

*T*his powerful song, which talks about the blessed promise our Lord gives us of His return, was written by Bill and
Gloria Gaither. I had the privilege of recording "The King
Is Coming" with Bill Walker, well-known as an arranger
and conductor in Nashville and New York.

The photo for the cover of the album by this title was
taken by Bud Meyer, a young ophthalmology student working his way through school. He captured on film a regally
spread dining room scene depicting the marriage supper of
the Lamb. Setting up a banquet table on top of a hotel
building in downtown Minneapolis, he borrowed ornate
chairs from the Calumet Hotel, obtained fine linen table
cloths, and used all the best silver and china. This young
man's vision was to try to impart to people the majesty and
awe of the bride (the church) sitting in Glory with the
Bridegroom (Jesus Christ).

At this beautiful banquet, I noticed there were no table
napkins. Would this be because there will be no spills, no
soiled hands? This is the banquet table of the King of kings!

The photographer was sensitive to the lighting, wanting
to capture just the right light as the sun was going down so
that the rays would shine over the beautiful scene.

It was a privilege for us to receive Bud Meyer's permission to use his photograph as it visually captures the heart of
the recording and the heart of the song "The King Is
Coming." The joyous expectation of each of us is to be
seated someday with the Lamb of God at the wedding feast
in heaven.

Coming for ME!

THE LORD HIMSELF WILL COME DOWN FROM HEAVEN, WITH
A LOUD COMMAND, WITH THE VOICE OF THE ARCHANGEL
AND WITH THE TRUMPET CALL OF GOD.

1 THESSALONIANS 4:16, NIV

I SAW A VAST CROWD, TOO GREAT TO COUNT, FROM EVERY
NATION AND TRIBE AND PEOPLE AND LANGUAGE, STANDING
IN FRONT OF THE THRONE AND BEFORE THE LAMB.

REVELATION 7:9, NLT

We love the triumphant music of loud trumpets and large choirs. However, nothing on earth will ever come close to the heavenly sound we'll hear someday when God calls us with His trumpet and "heaven's choir" begins to sing!

We don't know very much about heaven yet. But we do know that "there will be no more death or sorrow or crying or pain" (Revelation 21:4, NLT). That's enough reason to praise God and long for the time when all work will be "suspended as the King comes through the gate!"

Jesus, Lamb of God, I praise You for the promise that You will return to take me home with You. With great anticipation I wait for the wonderful wedding feast in heaven.

bfs

These Are the Things That Matter

A heart that's concerned for a fellow man,
An ear that will hear and will understand;
An eye that will look for the best in a man:
These are the things that matter.

A precious child that is yours to claim,
With trust in his eyes when he calls your name,
To live in a home and let love reign:
These are the things that matter.

To know that this life is for such a short time,
And to know there's a God and to know He's divine;
To know that He walks beside you all the time:
These are the things that matter.

Words and Music: Arthur Smith (b. 1922)
Copyright © 1957. Renewed 1978 by Clay Music Corporation,
5457 Monroe Road, P. O. Box 17551, Charlotte, NC 28211.
International copyright secured. All rights reserved. Used by permission.

These Are the Things That Matter

*W*ell-known on the country and pop charts for composing the instrumentals "Guitar Boogie" and "Dueling Banjos," Arthur Smith has been a country, bluegrass, and gospel musician for many years.

A radio personality since 1941, Arthur opened his first recording studio in 1951 in Charlotte, N.C. He went on to create and produce *The Arthur Smith Show,* an early-morning nationally syndicated telecast, that aired for twenty-one years. People still enjoy his wholesome entertainment, with spiritual emphasis, on public television.

My friendship with Arthur and his lovely wife, Dorothy, began in 1947 with their participation in the very first Billy Graham crusade held in Charlotte, North Carolina.

For some ten years, Arthur made his studio available for Mr. Graham's *Hour of Decision* program with Cliff Barrows and Grady Wilson.

Artists such as Johnny Cash, The Gatlin Brothers, The Gaithers, The Statler Brothers, The Blackwood Brothers, The Cathedrals, and numerous others have recorded Arthur Smith's inspirational compositions. I had the opportunity of recording for RCA and Word Records Arthur's songs "Acres of Diamonds," "I've Been with Jesus," "Tired of a Life Without Meaning," and "These Are the Things That Matter."

When Arthur's son Clay was born, he was so moved by another precious child coming into the home that he wanted to write a new song. Returning home from Atlanta by tour bus with his quartet, he wrote "These Are the Things That Matter."

Twenty-five years later, Arthur phoned me in Illinois and asked if I'd come to Charlotte and sing "These Are the Things That Matter" at Clay's wedding. What a privilege!

> *A precious child that is yours to claim,*
> *With trust in his eyes when he calls your name,*
> *To live in a home and let love reign:*
> *These are the things that matter.*

DEVOTIONAL INTERLUDE

Focusing on What's Most Important

CHILDREN ARE A GIFT FROM THE LORD; THEY ARE A REWARD FROM HIM.   PSALM 127:3, NLT

"OF ALL THE COMMANDMENTS, WHICH IS THE MOST IMPORTANT?" " '. . . LOVE THE LORD YOUR GOD WITH ALL YOUR HEART AND WITH ALL YOUR SOUL AND WITH ALL YOUR MIND AND WITH ALL YOUR STRENGTH.' THE SECOND IS THIS: 'LOVE YOUR NEIGHBOR AS YOURSELF.' THERE IS NO COMMANDMENT GREATER THAN THESE."   MARK 12:28-31, NIV

Sometimes a special event in our life will cause us to focus on our priorities. For Arthur Smith, that event was the birth of a son. He started thinking about how important it is to raise children in a Christian home, with love surrounding them. He knew that a parent's love helps a child learn to trust just as God's love helps us to trust Him. So he wrote about that love to illustrate what's most important in life.

Dear Lord, teach me how to show my love for You and for my family and friends, because I want to keep my focus on "the things that matter."

bfs

Wonderful Grace of Jesus

Wonderful grace of Jesus,
Greater than all my sin;
How shall my tongue describe it,
Where shall its praise begin?
Taking away my burden,
Setting my spirit free;
For the wonderful grace of Jesus reaches me.

Wonderful the matchless grace of Jesus,
Deeper than the mighty rolling sea;
Higher than the mountain, sparkling like a fountain,
All sufficient grace for even me;
Broader than the scope of my transgressions,
Greater far than all my sin and shame;
O magnify the precious name of Jesus,
Praise His name!

Wonderful grace of Jesus,
Reaching to all the lost,
By it I have been pardoned,
Saved to the uttermost;
Chains have been torn asunder,
Giving me liberty,
For the wonderful grace of Jesus reaches me.

Wonderful grace of Jesus,
Reaching the most defiled,
By its transforming power
Making me God's dear child,
Purchasing peace and heaven
For all eternity—
And the wonderful grace of Jesus reaches me.

Words and Music: Haldor Lillenas (1885–1959)

*H*aldor Lillenas, writer of "Wonderful Grace of Jesus,"
emigrated to America from Norway as a young child. He
became a pastor in the Church of the Nazarene and began
writing gospel songs, many of which were published in his
first book in the year 1919. In 1922, while still pastoring a
church, he formed the Lillenas Publishing Company. In
1930, the Nazarene Publishing House purchased his
company, which then became their music division.

Pastor Lillenas came for a week of preaching and singing
in my father's church in the New York area. Dad had
become acquainted with him through his reputation as a
fine preacher and songwriter. Mr. Lillenas was interested in
knowing that I was studying with the vocal coach, Manley
Price Boone, whose studio was atop the old Metropolitan
Opera building in New York.

Mr. Lillenas loved to tell stories, especially of his mission
trips to foreign countries. But he also told me about an
interesting incident in his own home. In the early days of
marriage, his wife was anxious to make sure that all doors
and windows were locked every night. After Mr. Lillenas
checked and double-checked the whole house, she would
still ask, "Did you check everywhere? Did you check behind
the doors?"

One night, after patiently acknowledging her questions
and making his rounds of the house, he was surprised to
find a large, disagreeable-looking character hiding behind
the bathroom door! Haldor said, "That man got by me and
ran down the stairs so fast, I couldn't catch him—not that I

wanted to! I shouted words I wished afterwards I hadn't. He took me by such surprise."

Haldor Lillenas had a love for life, and for allowing it to be lived to the fullest. He wrote lively songs of praise, such as "Wonderful Grace of Jesus."

An incident I fondly remember occurred when he accompanied me to a live early morning broadcast on a Jersey City radio station. As I started on the first solo, I found out that some hymns have two well-known tunes. The pianist started with one melody and I took the other! In my difficult situation I looked over at Mr. Lillenas, who already had his head in his hands, stifling a laugh. I motioned for immediate help. He jumped to the microphone and carried on, singing the hymn so beautifully with the same melody the pianist had chosen.

Thank you, Haldor Lillenas!

DEVOTIONAL INTERLUDE
Enjoying God's Grace

JESUS SAID, "IF YOU HOLD TO MY TEACHING, YOU ARE REALLY MY DISCIPLES. THEN YOU WILL KNOW THE TRUTH, AND THE TRUTH WILL SET YOU FREE. . . . IF THE SON SETS YOU FREE, YOU WILL BE FREE INDEED." JOHN 8:31-32, 36, NIV

Sometimes it seems as if we can't find enough superlatives to describe the way we feel about Jesus. That's when we go to a song like this one. The descriptive words, the bouncy rhythm, and the beautiful melody help us express how wonderful it is to know the truth of Jesus' grace, which frees us from our sins.

Jesus has purchased a place for us in heaven. What joy that puts into our life on this side of eternity as well as on the other side. Jesus' grace is "wonderful . . . greater than all my sin . . . matchless . . . all-sufficient . . . broader than the scope of my transgressions . . . transforming . . . greater far than all my sin and shame." So what will I do? I'll "magnify the precious name of Jesus!"

> *Lord Jesus, I give my burden of sin to You, for Your grace is more than sufficient to take it far away. I praise Your name, Jesus, for Your wonderful, "matchless grace."*

bfs

Songs Special to the Shea Family

$\mathcal{D}$ear Mr. Shea . . . My mother was born in Ottawa the summer of 1903 and orphaned at age eleven. The director of the orphanage where she was placed made sure the children were taken to church each Sunday. The pastor was your father, Rev. A. J. Shea. Until her death she had clear memories of her early visits to the manse. . . . We as a family have treasured your songs for years. We are also very grateful for your father reaching out to a little orphan girl and seeing her won to Christ.

—SALLY A., ARKANSAS, APRIL 2002

Adoration

My Jesus, Saviour, Friend, and glorious King,
Help me to praise Thee and help me to sing
Of Thy abounding grace and love to me,
Unworthy, poor, and sinful tho' I be.

O praise the Saviour, who from heaven came!
All that's within me bless His holy Name!
May Christ shine thru me, may my life be pure,
My eye be single and my footsteps sure.

Thy love is wonderful, Thy goodness great;
But may we not forget it till too late.
Oh, may none ever spurn Thy loving call,
But gladly yield to Thee, dear Lord, their all.

Words and Music: Maude Mary Shea (1881–1971)
Copyright © 1947 by George Beverly Shea. All rights reserved.

Adoration

There is no memory that is as special to me as the memory of my dear mother. She had a major influence on my life, sharing her love for the Lord and her love of music.

When Mother Shea was a young girl, musician and composer William O. Cushing was invited to preach at her father's church in Prescott, Ontario. During Mr. Cushing's visit to the Whitney home, my mother played the piano for him. Later in a letter he wrote from Painted Post, New York, "It was so nice to meet you and to hear you play the piano so well. I know that you are a little girl who loves the Lord."

Mr. Cushing composed the words to many old hymns, including "Follow On," "Hiding in Thee," "Ring the Bells of Heaven," "Under His Wings," and "When He Cometh." My sister Lois, who lives in New York, still has his kind letter, written in pencil, which so beautifully speaks of my mother's love for her Savior at an early age.

When Mother was twelve years old, she wrote the words and music to the hymn "Adoration." It expresses her mature faith even as a young girl. It was a faith that brought her so much peace and joy all of her ninety-one years.

There were eight of us children. Often when we'd see Mother rush through the room we would ask, "Mother, what is your *real* name?" With a smile, she would say, "My full name is Maude Mary Theodora Whitney Shea!" Laughingly, we would beg, "Say it again!" Then we would all laugh together.

It would be difficult to find words to express my deep appreciation for my mother. Even with her duties as the wife of a busy pastor, she always found time to be a loving counselor and guide to her eight children.

DEVOTIONAL INTERLUDE

Adoration

YOURS, O LORD, IS THE GREATNESS, THE POWER, THE
GLORY, THE VICTORY, AND THE MAJESTY. EVERYTHING IN
THE HEAVENS AND ON EARTH IS YOURS, O LORD, AND THIS
IS YOUR KINGDOM. WE ADORE YOU AS THE ONE WHO IS
OVER ALL THINGS.   I CHRONICLES 29:11, NLT

When we look at the greatness of the Lord described in
1 Chronicles 29, what better response could there be than
adoration? As Maude Mary Whitney recognized at age
twelve, this powerful Lord of the universe came to be our
"Saviour, Friend, and glorious King."

How grateful we are that this King extends His friendship to us even though we're "unworthy, poor, and sinful."
A wonderful prayer of response for each of us to pray is that
"my eye be single and my footsteps sure."

Ministering to those who "spurn" God's "loving call" is
a commendable single purpose for everyone to have. There
could be no better way to adore the Savior than to use the
gifts He has given us to bring others into the Kingdom.

> *My wonderful Jesus, how I adore You for all that You are
> and always will be. Your grace and love are beyond my
> comprehension. But I accept these gifts from You and offer
> my adoration in return.*

bfs

Blessing for Food

As sung in the Adam and Maude Mary Shea home around the table, to
the tune of "The Doxology"

We thank Thee, Lord, for this our food,
But more because of Jesus' love
This manna bless and grant that we
May feast in paradise with Thee.
Amen

As printed on a teapot presented to John Wesley in 1761 by
Josiah Wedgwood; words credited to John Cennick (1718–1755)

Be present at our Table, Lord.
Be here and everywhere ador'd.
These creatures bless and grant that we
May feast in paradise with Thee.

We thank Thee, Lord, for this our food,
But more because of Jesus' love
Let manna to our Souls be given,
The Bread of Life sent down from Heaven.

From an old Methodist prayer book

Be present at our table, Lord.
Be here and everywhere adored.
These mercies bless and grant that we
May feast in paradise with Thee.

We thank Thee, Lord, for this our food,
We thank Thee more for Jesus' blood.
Let manna to our souls be given,
The Bread of Life sent down from Heaven.
Amen

I grew up in a family of eight children. So even when my two oldest siblings went away to school, there were still six of us children around the table for meals.

There was prayer at the table three times a day—each was a very brief prayer led by Dad, Mother, or one of the children. On special occasions my mother liked to have us sing the blessing for the food.

The song we sang was based on a table prayer written many years ago and handed down from one generation to the next. There are many variations of this simple little prayer.

The tune is the "Old Hundredth," which is the melody most often used in churches for "The Doxology." In my family we would sing the blessing for the food in unison. Then we'd repeat it, breaking into harmony, with Dad singing bass. It's a wonderful memory!

In the evening my father would read to the family the Scripture he had chosen for that day, usually very brief because of the young children. He would read verses that might help us deal with an issue we had been discussing. Or sometimes the Scripture would help us survive a difficulty we were going through at the time. Then we'd sing together around the table. Of course, this was long before television sets came into our homes.

Music was an important part of family life as I was growing up. It brought us together, reaping eternal benefits. I am so thankful to my parents for living their faith before us and loving us into it.

My parents' faith became a reality in each of their children's lives. Pauline is a Nazarene pastor's wife. Dr. Whitney Shea is a professor at Houghton College and World War II veteran, and his wife, Phoebe, a former comptroller at Houghton. Mary is a Wesleyan pastor's wife. Next comes "Bev," privileged to be a gospel singer and now married to Karlene, a former assistant in Mr. Graham's North Carolina office. The Rev. Alton Shea is a Methodist pastor and missionary and is married to Aileen Ortlip (Shea), a well-known portrait artist most recently commissioned to do the portraits of six college presidents. Lois is the wife of Dr. Kenneth Wright, physician and World War II veteran. Ruth is a teacher, married to Houghton College professor and World War II veteran Dr. Edward Willett. Grace is married to Bill Baker, electronic engineer and World War II naval veteran.

Family Prayer Time

HE GAVE YOU FOOD SO YOU WOULD KNOW THAT HE IS THE
LORD YOUR GOD.   DEUTERONOMY 29:6, NLT

GIVE US THIS DAY OUR DAILY BREAD.   MATTHEW 6:11, KJV

God never tires of finding ways to give us what we need. He
sent manna to the Israelites in the wilderness. And He sends
us our daily bread. God also sent us Jesus, who is the Bread
of Life. Jesus set the precedent for table prayers when He
asked God to bless the food with which He fed over five
thousand people (Matthew 14:19).

Today, finding a time when the family can be together
for meals is difficult because of busy schedules. But mealtime is the perfect place to develop family values and to
bond with one another and with God.

*I love You, Lord, and I thank You for the food You
provide. I know that mealtime is a great time to talk with
You and with my family. While it may not be possible for
my whole family to be together at every meal, I thank You
for the fellowship we enjoy whenever we do share a meal
together.*

bfs

He Died of a Broken Heart

Also known as "The Broken Heart"

Have you read the story of the Cross
Where Jesus bled and died;
Where your debt was paid by His precious blood
That gushed from His wounded side?

He died of a broken heart for thee,
He died of a broken heart.
Oh, wondrous love! It was for thee,
He died of a broken heart.

Have you read how they placed the crown of thorns
Upon His lovely brow,
When He prayed, "Forgive them, oh! forgive;
They know not what they do"?

Have you read that He saved the dying thief,
When hanging on the tree,
Who looked with pitying eyes and said,
"Dear Lord, remember me"?

Have you read that He looked to heav'n
And said, "It's finished—'twas for thee"?
Have you ever said, "I thank Thee, Lord,
For giving Thy life for me"?

Words and Music: Thomas Dennis

I have such happy memories of my family's evangelist friend Fred Suffield and his songwriter wife, Kittie. They were of great encouragement to me.

It was my seventeenth summer and I was with the Suffields at their tent meetings in the Rideau Lake Country of Westport, Ontario. Rev. Fred was a humble man—he proved this to me on a Sunday morning when I arrived at their tent to walk with them to the service. I noticed my shoes were dusty and asked Mr. Suffield if he had a brush handy. He said, "Put your foot up here!" "Oh, no," I said. But he insisted. And it was then that the preacher of the morning shined my shoes! I remember this as a lesson in humility.

Kittie gently said to me one day, "You know, Bev, you will have to get on your feet and sing your first solo at one of our meetings. I'll be there to help you at the piano."

Well, the song we chose for that first solo was "He Died of a Broken Heart." It seemed to be going well, but in the second verse I noticed my voice cracked, and I was rather embarrassed.

At breakfast the next morning, Kittie told me not to worry. Next time she would just transpose the music into a lower key.

"He Died of a Broken Heart" was printed in a collection of songs by Homer Rodeheaver. (For many years, Homer was the soloist and song leader for Billy Sunday's evangelistic meetings.) I still enjoy looking at that old songbook where underlined in red ink are some of the tender words:

Oh, wondrous love! It was for thee,
He died of a broken heart.

At the 2002 Winchester, Ontario, hometown event we were pleased to have a former Canadian Mountie, Mr. Garth Hampson, as the Master of Ceremonies.

Just before we went to the platform, I told my new friend how, as a young man of eighteen, I had admired the beautiful red coats and skilled horsemanship of the Mounties who served in the daily changing of the guard before the House of Parliament. Already standing at six-foot-two inches, I had pictured how much taller I would stand in a Mountie uniform with the red coat and classic Mountie hat. I had even gone to the recruitment office and begun to fill out the application. But in the middle of filling out the questionnaire, I had a chilling thought: *Maybe they won't assign me to the Parliament guard and I'll find myself instead on a horse in the Northwest Territories.*

Sheepishly folding the application, I slipped it into my pocket, and that was as close as I came to a career with the Royal Canadian Mounted Police.

As I related this tale to Mr. Hampson, he laughed and said to me, "You were exactly right about the possibility of having to serve in the Northwest Territories. I spent the first ten years doing just that. But for me, it proved to be a fine assignment."

When he retired, the RCMP graciously extended to Mr. Hampson the opportunity to represent this highly respected law enforcement agency in travels worldwide as a singing goodwill ambassador.

At that Sunday afternoon concert in Winchester, Mr. Hampson paused before singing to say, "I am holding in my hand the music of the first solo that Bev ever sang, at age seventeen, in nearby Westport, Ontario. It is my privilege to sing it for you."

Hearing Mr. Hampson sing this song seventy-six years later, it is evident that the wonderful message of this hymn is as relevant today as when it was written long ago.

Garth Hampson's rich, lyric tenor voice was full of pathos and tender vocal shading. It touched my heart deeply, along with the hearts of four thousand people present. After finishing, he went over to his chair, picked up the famous Mountie hat, and with a big smile he firmly placed it on my head—to keep forever. Today that hat is displayed in a place of honor in our North Carolina home, irresistably tried on by most every visitor!

Jesus' Died for Me

Jesus said, "It is finished." With that, he bowed his head and gave up his spirit. John 19:30, NIV

Jesus' last hours before His death were filled with pain and sadness; but instead of focusing on Himself, He turned His attention to those around Him. While He was enduring physical, emotional, and spiritual trauma, Jesus was exhibiting concern and compassion for others. He offered forgiveness to a criminal, as well as to those who were crucifying Him. If Jesus was willing to forgive those people at the Cross, we know He is willing to forgive us.

The most significant cause of Jesus' heart being broken was our sins. Those sins saddened Him and made Him willing to die for us so we could be forgiven.

Lord Jesus, thank You for giving Your life for me. I know it was Your love and compassion that made You willing to die "of a broken heart." Please help me now to be Your faithful follower.

bfs

Singing I Go

The trusting heart to Jesus clings,
Nor any ill forebodes,
But at the cross of Calv'ry, sings,
Praise God for lifted loads!

Singing I go along life's road,
Praising the Lord, praising the Lord,
Singing I go along life's road,
For Jesus has lifted my load.

The passing days bring many cares,
"Fear not," I hear Him say,
And when my fears are turned to prayers,
The burdens slip away.

He tells me of my Father's love,
And never slumb'ring eye,
My everlasting King above
Will all my needs supply.

When to the throne of grace I flee,
I find the promise true,
The mighty arms upholding me
Will bear my burdens too.

Words: Eliza E. Hewitt (1851–1920)
Music: William J. Kirkpatrick (1838–1921)

"Singing I Go" brings back fond memories from my childhood. At the Shea home we called this spirited old song "Mother's alarm clock for her children."

Early in the morning of most school days, we would hear the chord in the key of E major on the Bell upright piano. Then Mother would begin singing this chorus:

Singing I go along life's road,
Praising the Lord, praising the Lord,
Singing I go along life's road,
For Jesus has lifted my load.

She would follow her wake-up song with cheerful words such as, "Get up, everybody. One hour till school!" Oh, yes, that was the way of life in our home.

Six of the eight Shea children were born during my father's first pastorate in Winchester, Ontario. I remember Dad renting part of a boxcar from the Canadian Pacific Railroad and loading in the family piano and furniture. We were told how it would make its way across the St. Lawrence River on a car ferry to Rochester, New York. There the boxcar would be transferred to the Pennsylvania Railroad, then ride the rails to Houghton, New York. Here the children were able to enroll in the Houghton Christian Academy, and again each morning we awoke to the words of "Singing I Go." Four years later, we moved back to Ottawa, Ontario, to a new pastorate. Our piano came along and our mother was still awakening us with "Singing I Go." In the early 1930s, we returned to the United States, moving to Jersey City, New Jersey, right on the Hudson River, across from New York City. In each parsonage we were still hearing the "wake-up song."

Years later, I was invited to become a radio announcer and singer for the Moody Bible Institute radio station, WMBI, in Chicago. I started a morning program called *Hymns from the Chapel*, and the theme was "Singing I Go."

In 1943, Billy Graham, a student at nearby Wheaton College, heard the program, visited our studios, and extended an invitation for me to join him on his own new radio broadcast, *Songs in the Night*. That was just the beginning of our lifetime of working together. He was then twenty-one and I was thirty-one; the age difference remains to this day!

For eight years, I hosted a radio show of hymns on ABC, *Club Time*, sponsored by Club Aluminum. Don Hustad, later a member of the Billy Graham team, was musical director of the show. Its theme song was "Singing I Go." Each week we featured a favorite hymn of a famous person. Babe Ruth's favorite was "God Is Ever Beside Me." Kate Smith's was "I Love to Tell the Story," and American baritone John Charles Thomas liked "Softly and Tenderly."

During World War II, the Armed Forces Network asked ABC if they could rebroadcast the program on their stations. The show's theme song was "Singing I Go," and Mother's wake-up song was now traveling around the globe.

May I mention Mother's Bell piano again? It is now all of one hundred years old, tuned three times a year, and gently cared for in the Syracuse home of my sister Lois. On this piano I wrote the music to "I'd Rather Have Jesus."

DEVOTIONAL INTERLUDE

Many Reasons to Sing

PRAISE BE TO THE LORD, TO GOD OUR SAVIOR, WHO DAILY
BEARS OUR BURDENS.   PSALM 68:19, NIV

SHOUT FOR JOY TO THE LORD, ALL THE EARTH, BURST INTO
JUBILANT SONG WITH MUSIC; MAKE MUSIC TO THE LORD
WITH THE HARP, WITH THE HARP AND THE SOUND OF
SINGING.   PSALM 98:4-5, NIV

Mrs. Adam (Maude) Shea, being a pastor's wife and caring
for her eight children, had her share of cares, burdens, and
heavy loads. But she chose an uplifting song to be an
encouragement to her family—and to herself.

Jesus, the great lifter of all loads, can put a song in every
heart that trusts in Him. When our fears, which are often
related to our cares, "are turned to prayers, the burdens slip
away."

While our "life's road" is not always smooth or straight,
we can still sing and praise the Lord along the rough spots
and around the curves. He has lifted our load!

Thank You, Lord, for the loads You have lifted. Forgive
me for times when I've focused on my cares instead of on
Your ability to handle them. Help me to keep singing and
praising You, wherever "life's road" leads.

bfs

Welcome, Welcome

Welcome, welcome, welcome, welcome!
Holy Ghost, we welcome Thee.
Come in power and fill this temple;
Holy Ghost, we welcome Thee.
(Repeat)

Words: Leila N. Morris (1862–1929)
Music: Daniel Read (1757–1836)

Welcome, Welcome

I was invited to a sacred music conference in Dallas, Texas. Some ten or twelve choir directors and musicians had gathered with Bill and Gloria Gaither around a refreshment table one night after the evening meeting. Gloria Gaither suggested we each recount an early hymn or gospel song that had remained dear to our hearts since childhood. I shared the following story.

As a young boy in my father's small church in Winchester, Ontario, I often heard him say to the people who were gathering before the service on Sunday morning, "Friends, there are a few minutes before the meeting gets underway. Perhaps some of you would like to gather with me around the altar for quiet prayer and meditation." Someone would begin to sing softly this old hymn, and although I was but a small boy, this is one of my forever memories. As the worshipers would repeat the refrain, I could hear soft harmonies and the richness of the voices together in song and fervent prayer.

In the telling of this story I began to sing this tender song:

*W*elcome, welcome, welcome, welcome!
Holy Ghost, we welcome Thee.
Come in power and fill this temple;
Holy Ghost, we welcome Thee.

Each one gathered there at the table in Dallas seemed warmly touched by this story, and there were even a few moist eyes.

The late Fred Bock, a friend who was choir director and

organist at Hollywood Presbyterian Church in California, had a choir arrangement made of this song. He would have his choir sing softly, "Welcome, Welcome," perhaps once a month at the start of their morning service.

We have been hearing of people around the nation singing this song from time to time in the opening moments of the morning worship.

My daughter Elaine's pastor, having heard her sing "Welcome, Welcome," sometimes would call her during the week and say, "Sunday morning, Elaine." Taking her place at the top of the gallery she would note the pastor's nod and begin to sing a cappella in her beautiful contralto voice. The music seemed to echo down on the worshipers below, "Welcome, welcome! Holy Ghost, we welcome Thee."

DEVOTIONAL INTERLUDE

Our Comforter and Truth Provider

I WILL PRAY THE FATHER, AND HE SHALL GIVE YOU ANOTHER
COMFORTER, THAT HE MAY ABIDE WITH YOU FOR EVER; EVEN
THE SPIRIT OF TRUTH; WHOM THE WORLD CANNOT RECEIVE,
BECAUSE IT SEETH HIM NOT, NEITHER KNOWETH HIM: BUT
YE KNOW HIM; FOR HE DWELLETH WITH YOU, AND SHALL BE
IN YOU. I WILL NOT LEAVE YOU COMFORTLESS: I WILL COME
TO YOU. . . . THE COMFORTER, WHICH IS THE HOLY GHOST,
WHOM THE FATHER WILL SEND IN MY NAME, HE SHALL
TEACH YOU ALL THINGS, AND BRING ALL THINGS TO YOUR
REMEMBRANCE, WHATSOEVER I HAVE SAID UNTO YOU.

JOHN 14:16–18, 26, KJV

WHEN HE, THE SPIRIT OF TRUTH, COMES, HE WILL GUIDE
YOU INTO ALL TRUTH. HE WILL NOT SPEAK ON HIS OWN; HE
WILL SPEAK ONLY WHAT HE HEARS, AND HE WILL TELL YOU
WHAT IS YET TO COME. JOHN 16:13, NIV

Nothing today could equal the experience of those who
followed Jesus while He walked on this earth. However,
Jesus has kept His promise not to abandon His followers.
He has given us the very special gift of the third Person of
the Trinity. The Holy Spirit is available to bring each of us
comfort and to teach us what is true. We are not alone!

> *Holy Spirit, I welcome You and ask for Your daily coun-*
> *sel, encouragement, comfort, and guidance. Fill every*
> *temple with power, enabling us to worship in spirit*
> *and in truth.*

bfs

When I've Gone the Last Mile

Also known as "The Last Mile of the Way"

If I walk in the pathway of duty,
If I work till the close of the day,
I shall see the great king in His beauty
When I've gone the last mile of the way.

When I've gone the last mile of the way,
I will rest at the close of the day.
And I know there are joys that await me
When I've gone the last mile of the way.

If for Christ I proclaim the glad story,
If I seek for His sheep gone astray,
I am sure He will show me His glory
When I've gone the last mile of the way.

Here the dearest of ties we must sever,
Tears of sorrow are seen every day,
But no sickness, no sighing for ever
When I've gone the last mile of the way.

And if here I have earnestly striven,
And have tried all His will to obey,
'Twill enhance all the rapture of heaven
When I've gone the last mile of the way.

Words: Johnson Oatman, Jr. (1856–1922)
Music: William E. Marks

The Reverend George Whitney, my maternal grandfather and the man for whom I was named, was a wonderful man who served God all of his life.

As I was growing up, I often heard the story of how my father, Adam Joseph Shea, met Grandfather Whitney in Prescott, on the banks of the St. Lawrence River in Ontario, Canada. Dad grew up in a home that was supposed to be religious, but his father's lifestyle was not Christian. This turned my father away from Christianity. However, John Scobie, an evangelist, preached a captivating message that led my father to give his heart to the Lord.

John Scobie stayed in touch with my father for a number of years and encouraged him to contact the Rev. George Whitney. Scobie knew that Mr. Whitney was like a one-man seminary. Well, Adam Shea went to see George Whitney and began visiting him every week, and he learned more about the Scriptures. He also learned there was a daughter in the home, Maude Mary, who eventually became Adam Shea's wife and my mother!

I was five when Grandfather Whitney reached retirement age. However, hearing of the need for a pastor in a small country church in Marengo, Iowa, my grandparents moved from Ontario, Canada. As a family, we traveled by train in 1913 to visit the Whitneys at Christmastime. This meant changing trains and sleeping for a night on the oak benches of Union Station in Chicago. We four children thought this was a great adventure, especially when a horse-drawn streetcar carried us from one train station to the other. That Christmas, I received a little black iron locomotive from my grandfather. I treasured this.

A short time later, my grandfather suffered from heart failure. The doctor called on him in his home and was not surprised to find him singing. "George, you can't do this; it takes strength to sing like you do," said the doctor. "I know you are a man of song, but this is hard on you because you are too passionate about it." Well, singing was one of the things Grandfather enjoyed doing, in the home, or while out in the buggy. It was how he worshiped and showed love for our Lord Jesus. Some time later, after the physician had cautioned him, my grandmother again heard him singing, because he just couldn't contain all that he felt within:

When I've gone the last mile of the way,
I will rest at the close of the day.
And I know there are joys that await me . . .

Grandfather went to be with the Lord before he could finish the verse, "When I've gone the last mile of the way."

Johnson Oatman, composer of this hymn-song, also wrote the words to "Count Your Blessings." What greater blessing could there be than to know we will be with Jesus at the end of the journey!

My father, who had learned so much from his father-in-law, also loved the hymns of the church. Dad suffered many weeks of illness. Early on Thanksgiving morning in 1946, my sister came into the room to be with him. He looked at her and asked, "Pauline, do you hear the music?" "What music, Papa?" and she heard in an almost inaudible voice, "Oh, you wouldn't know."

About an hour later, my father was in his eternal home

with the Lord Jesus. He had served as a pastor for fifty-three years, loving people and adoring Mother and all of his eight children, with affection never ending.

Scripture says, "Are not all angels ministering spirits sent to serve those who will inherit salvation?" (Hebrews 1:14, NIV). Billy Graham wrote, "In that last moment—the greatest crisis of all—He will have His angels gather you in their arms to carry you gloriously, wonderfully into heaven."[5]

Today so many of us know dear ones and friends who have "gone the last mile of the way." While we feel the loss of their presence here, Scripture assures us that those who have gone before are enjoying the glories of heaven.

---

[5]*Angels: God's Secret Agents*, Billy Graham, Doubleday & Company, Inc., New York, 1975, p. 155.

DEVOTIONAL INTERLUDE

Walking Every Mile with Jesus

LET US RUN WITH PERSEVERANCE THE RACE MARKED OUT FOR US. LET US FIX OUR EYES ON JESUS, THE AUTHOR AND PERFECTER OF OUR FAITH.   HEBREWS 12:1-2, NIV

BEHOLD, I AM COMING SOON! MY REWARD IS WITH ME, AND I WILL GIVE TO EVERYONE ACCORDING TO WHAT HE HAS DONE.   REVELATION 22:12, NIV

Many Scripture passages refer to the importance of serving the Lord all our days and persevering in the race God has set before us. What's important to remember is that Christ empowers us to do His work. He tells us, "My power is made perfect in weakness" (2 Corinthians 12:9, NIV). The more we recognize our weaknesses and depend on His strength, the stronger we become!

After we accept the wonderful salvation that God offers us, what a privilege it is to show our thankfulness through obedience and service. We won't know until we've "gone the last mile" just how great our reward will be for faithfully following our Savior.

Lord Jesus, I want to walk every mile with You. Thank You for giving me the strength to do Your will.

bfs

Blue Galilee

I stood by the side of the murmuring sea
Of Galilee, blue Galilee,
When the sunshine its beauty revealed unto me,
Blue Galilee, sweet Galilee;
Then I tho't of my Saviour who, years long ago,
Came to tell the glad story His love to bestow,
As He stood by the side of that murmuring sea
Of Galilee, blue Galilee.

I sailed in a ship on that billowy sea
Of Galilee, blue Galilee,
While the voice of the tempest was saying to me,
Blue Galilee, sweet Galilee;
Then I tho't of the hearts who once tossed on
    the wave,
When they cried in their peril to Him who could
    save,
How the Master spoke peace to that billowy sea
Of Galilee, blue Galilee.

I love to recall the bright silvery sea
Of Galilee, blue Galilee,
For its wonderful story is precious to me,
Blue Galilee, sweet Galilee;
As it tells of my Saviour who came from above,
With the treasures of mercy and infinite love,
Standing there by the side of that silvery sea
Of Galilee, blue Galilee.

Words: Neal A. McAuley
Music: George Beverly Shea (b. 1909)

I have stood by the Sea of Galilee and traveled across the lake in a hundred-foot sight-seeing launch. It's difficult to describe the emotions that arise during such an experience. I found myself recalling many Bible stories from childhood that refer to Jesus being in this area.

The words to "Blue Galilee" were written many years ago, and I added the music in 1947. One of the greatest thrills was being able to sing the words to this song while crossing the Sea of Galilee. The Jewish boat captain asked for a copy of the song, which I was pleased to give him. I was with Roy Gustafson, one of the associate evangelists on our team. Roy led over 150 Bible study tours to the Holy Land, on which he taught history and prophecy.

On April 16, 2002, I sang the song for Roy Gustafson for the last time. The occasion was this eighty-seven-year-old preacher's memorial service at The Cove, the Billy Graham training center in Asheville, North Carolina.

Mr. Gustafson joined the team in 1959, but he and Mr. Graham had been friends ever since they were students at the Florida Bible Institute. When Billy Graham's son Franklin was a teenager, he worked with Roy Gustafson on many of his summer tours to the Middle East. Franklin says that it was through Roy that he first felt called into ministry. Then, at the age of twenty-two, Franklin was with Roy on his last summer tour. It was during that summer when Franklin, who had been living a rebellious life, chose to stop running from the Lord. We now rejoice in his extensive ministry with Samaritan's Purse and World Medical Mission.

I recall one time when eighty-nine people on Roy Gustafson's tour were staying at Hotel Capernaum. While Roy was speaking in the lobby, some of the local Jewish people were listening. It happened again the next day. They were intrigued by his words because they could tell that he knew the history of the land well.

The Israeli government has a tree-lined street, a memorial to people who have honored Israel. A tree has been planted in Mr. Gustafson's name because of his love for the land, his knowledge, and his encouragement to others to visit this wonderful country, the birthplace of our Lord.

Thinking about Jesus by Galilee

ONE DAY AS JESUS WAS PREACHING ON THE SHORE OF THE SEA OF GALILEE, GREAT CROWDS PRESSED IN ON HIM TO LISTEN TO THE WORD OF GOD. . . . WHEN HE HAD FINISHED SPEAKING, HE SAID TO SIMON, "NOW GO OUT WHERE IT IS DEEPER AND LET DOWN YOUR NETS, AND YOU WILL CATCH MANY FISH." LUKE 5:1-4, NLT

How grateful we are that Jesus walked on earth and sailed on the blue waters of Galilee. As we recall the lessons He taught and the miracles He performed in this area, we appreciate the love that brought Him to us.

As recorded in Psalm 122, King David challenges us to pray for the Holy Land, where our Lord spent over thirty years: "Pray for the peace of Jerusalem. May all who love this city prosper" (verse 6). And in Isaiah 65, Isaiah reminds us of God's promise to create "new heavens and a new earth. . . . I will create Jerusalem as a place of happiness. Her people will be a source of joy" (Isaiah 65:17-18).

Heavenly Father, thank You for sending Your Son to the land of Israel to teach us about You. We pray for peace in Jerusalem, and we look forward to the day when Jesus will return, taking us with Him to live in the new Jerusalem for eternity.

bfs

I'd Rather Have Jesus

I'd rather have Jesus than silver or gold;
I'd rather be His than have riches untold:
I'd rather have Jesus than houses or lands.
I'd rather be led by His nail-pierced hand . . .

Then to be the king of a vast domain
Or be held in sin's dread sway.
I'd rather have Jesus than anything
This world affords today.

I'd rather have Jesus than men's applause;
I'd rather be faithful to His dear cause;
I'd rather have Jesus than worldwide fame.
I'd rather be true to His holy name . . .

He's fairer than lilies of rarest bloom;
He's sweeter than honey from out the comb;
He's all that my hungering spirit needs.
I'd rather have Jesus and let Him lead . . .

Words: Rhea F. Miller (1894–1966)
Music: George Beverly Shea (b. 1909)
Copyright © 1922. Renewed 1950. Music copyright © 1939 by
Word Music, Inc. All rights reserved. Used by permission.

*A*s mentioned in the story "Go Down, Moses," I met
Fred Allen and was on the amateur portion of his program
on NBC coast to coast. It was a great experience, but I felt a
certain uneasiness that this was not right for me to pursue.
This was a special time with important choices to make,
choices that could affect the rest of my life.

At the age of twenty-three, I was living at home with
my parents, continuing to work at Mutual Life and studying
voice with Manley Price Boone, traveling by subway and the
Hudson River ferry every day. Going to the piano one
Sunday morning, I found a poem waiting for me there. I
recognized my mother's handwriting. She had copied the
words of a poem by Rhea F. Miller, knowing her son would
read the beautiful message, which speaks of *choice*. As I read
these precious words: "I'd rather have Jesus than men's
applause; I'd rather be faithful to His dear cause," I found
myself singing the words in a melody that expressed the feelings of my heart. What a joy it was to sing with fervent
voice in the key of B-flat:

*Than to be the king of a vast domain
Or be held in sin's dread sway.
I'd rather have Jesus than anything
This world affords today.*

Soon a mother's arms were around my shoulders. She
had been in the next room having her devotions and now,

joining me at the piano, there were tears in her eyes. She knew the words were having the desired effect—they were speaking to me about life's choices.

The Better Choice

A few years later, in 1936, I had an opportunity to audition for CBS. At the time, a friend and I were singing in the choir at Calvary Baptist Church, right across from Carnegie Hall. We learned that twenty-five new voices were being considered to tour and perform on national radio with Lynn Murray's singing group.

Arriving at the audition, I was really quite nervous. When it was my turn I sang, "I am going down to the river; oh, yes, I'm going down to the river," with a big "Old Man River" climax.

Then Mr. Murray gave me another song to learn. He told me to come back in a week. I delayed a little. Reading the words to the song, it just didn't seem to fit with what I wanted to do in music and song. The very thought of it brought an ache to the soul, and I had a feeling within that seemed to say, *Don't go any further with this.*

The secretary called back to say that I had been chosen without further need to return. I thanked her but explained that I had decided to stay in office work and continue vocal instruction.

I continued working at the insurance company, enjoying the music and vocal instruction each week.

The words *I'd rather have Jesus* had sunk deep into my heart. I knew that following Him was more important than having "men's applause" or "worldwide fame."

THE SONG IS PUBLISHED

Soon New York was left behind. I was offered the position of singer and announcer at WMBI in Chicago, the Christian radio station originating from the Moody Bible Institute. Once in Chicago, I remembered that Rhea F. Miller, writer of the beautiful poem, was the wife of a Nazarene pastor in the Chicago area. Making an appointment, I visted with them in their south Chicago home.

Mrs. Miller was aware of the new music I had written for her poem "I'd Rather Have Jesus." I had been singing the song on WMBI radio, and people had been inquiring about it. Mrs. Miller and her husband, Dr. Howard V. Miller (who later became a well-known superintendent of the Nazarene Church), agreed to help me get the song published.

At that time, a steel plate of the four-part harmony, music, and words was created. It was hymnbook-sized and used to make copies—a keepsake I'd love to have in hand today. I never dreamed this song would be translated into so many languages.

PRESIDENT EISENHOWER

In the 1950s there was a gathering of twelve hundred young people in the Mayflower Hotel Ballroom in Washington, D. C. President Eisenhower was to address the group immediately following Cliff Barrows's inspiring message. I had the privilege of singing.

Before Cliff had finished his message, a Secret Service man came with the presidential seal, which as you know always has to be placed in front of the president of the United States when he speaks. Right in front of the lectern while Cliff was speaking, this man hammered the seal into place. *Bang, bang!* Cliff chuckled and realized he needed to end in a hurry!

The president arrived, and Dr. Daniel Poling, who at that time was editor of *Christian Herald* magazine, warmly and enthusiastically introduced him. The president talked for several minutes to the young people. When he had finished, Dr. Poling asked if he could remain a few more minutes. "Oh, yes. I'd like to," came the response.

I was sitting way at the back of the platform when Dr. Poling indicated it was my time to sing "I'd Rather Have Jesus." Tedd Smith was at the piano. Later, as the president was leaving, he came to shake my hand and said, "Thank you for that song." That short sentence seemed to say to me that the president of the United States really understood the meaning of faith in the Lord Jesus.

WORLD WAR II

After World War II, I received a letter from a GI, a wonderful young organist whose musical studies were interrupted by the war. He was with the troops occupying a village in France after it had been severely bombed by the enemy. Crushed to see that a church had been partially demolished, he was immediately concerned about the organ. Climbing through the rubble, he wondered about the instrument. He found it! Sitting at the console, he pushed a button and the huge four-manual organ came to life! In a moment he was playing over and over, "I'd Rather Have Jesus." The rich music of this beautiful organ rose above the ruin and desolation of the war-torn village.

What a precious letter from this young man.

The King and Queen of England

King George VI and the Queen of England were visiting President and Mrs. Roosevelt in the White House. The queen later became known to us as the Queen Mother after her husband passed away and her daughter Elizabeth ascended the throne. The Queen Mother lived to be 101, as you may recall, passing away in 2002.

On that particular visit to the United States, a well-known Native American opera singer, Chief Whitefeather, was invited to sing for the king and queen and President and Mrs. Roosevelt. After singing two operatic arias, for which his small audience showed great appreciation, the chief asked, "May I sing something from deep within my heart?"

Soon they were hearing the beautiful words of "I'd Rather Have Jesus." When he finished, in the silence of the moment, the queen said to him, "This song bespeaks the sentiment of my heart—and that of my husband."

Some thirty years later Bishop Michael Baughen of All Souls Langham Place, London, was to speak at the chapel attended by the Queen Mother, so loved by the people of England. Bishop Baughen, having heard this story of Chief Whitefeather singing "I'd Rather Have Jesus" at the White House wrote to the secretary of the Queen Mother and asked for permission to include the incident in his sermon. It was reported that she remembered, and the story was told again.

In Other Languages

During a recent evening of song I was telling people of the origins of "I'd Rather Have Jesus." I told how I endeavor to sing this song in several languages. With a chuckle I started to sing what I remembered of the Japanese version.

At the close of the evening, a young couple rushed to tell me that they were hosts to a newly arrived Japanese family who had never been to church. They were surprised and touched to hear about Jesus through a song in their very own language.

I've had the challenge of singing this song in all of Mr. Graham's crusades around the globe—in Mandarin, Swedish, Finnish, Spanish, and Japanese. How precious it is to know how God has used these beautiful lyrics, penned long ago by Rhea F. Miller, to touch lives.

From Tanzania

Letter from Christy Shea (a missionary in Tanzania) to her uncle:

Dear Uncle Bev,

I wanted to share with you that a few weeks ago I attended a street-side church service for homeless people. Most of them had leprosy. They sat along the curb of the street over a gutter, with their cardboard homes on the sidewalk behind our backs.

The choir got up to sing—most of them missing fingers or toes. They sang the song to which you wrote the music, "I'd Rather Have Jesus," in the Swahili language. It made a big impact on me to hear them singing. In spite of the state of their lives, they sang it with all their hearts.

DEVOTIONAL INTERLUDE

Having Jesus

I HAD RATHER BE A DOORKEEPER IN THE HOUSE OF MY GOD,
THAN TO DWELL IN THE TENTS OF WICKEDNESS.

PSALM 84:10, KJV

EVERYTHING ELSE IS WORTHLESS WHEN COMPARED WITH
THE PRICELESS GAIN OF KNOWING CHRIST JESUS MY LORD.
I HAVE DISCARDED EVERYTHING ELSE, COUNTING IT ALL AS
GARBAGE, SO THAT I MAY HAVE CHRIST AND BECOME ONE
WITH HIM. PHILIPPIANS 3:8-9, NLT

Because of the great appreciation that's been expressed over
the years for Mrs. Miller's poem, it's clear that many people
truly would "rather have Jesus" than anything else. We read
ads and listen to commercials that try to convince us we
can't do without a multitude of products. Nevertheless,
many of us realize that while we can do without "things,"
the truth is that we really do need Jesus.

> *Lord Jesus, You are "fairer than lilies" and "sweeter than
> honey." I'd rather have You as my Savior and Friend than
> receive any gift that money can buy. I'd rather have You
> than _____ or anything else "this world affords
> today."*

bfs

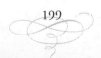

I Love Thy Presence, Lord

I love Thy presence, Lord,
The place of secret prayer;
My soul communes with Thee,
And gone is earthly care.
I love Thy presence, Lord;
To me Thou art made real,
As when on Galilean hills,
Thy loving touch didst heal.

I see Thy nail-scarred hands,
Outstretched in love to me;
I know Thou'rt working still,
Thy hidden plan I see.
I love Thy presence, Lord,
This very present pow'r
That makes me know my pray'rs
Are heard in heav'n this very hour.

Words: Alton J. Shea
Music: George Beverly Shea (b. 1909)

*I*t was wartime in 1944, the middle of a decade when I became weighed down with anxieties. Yet it was during this period of my life that I also found prayer time more and more meaningful.

We were a young couple with two small children. My three sisters had husbands in the service, and my brother Dr. Whitney Shea also was called to duty for Uncle Sam. Rationing was in force, salaries were limited, and burdens became heavy for many people.

Then one day I recall sitting beside the radio, listening to the news and pondering, *If reports can be heralded across the world like that, then prayer must be more powerful still. God will hear our prayers.*

My anxieties gave way to a sense of peace as the fact of the heavenly Father's care became a living reality. And the words of a simple couplet seemed to come so easily: "My soul communes with Thee/And gone is earthly care."

It is possible to live on the bright side of difficulties by offering to God believing and persistent prayers. Doing this calls for a quiet time, a quiet place, and a quiet heart to hear the still, small voice of God. But it brings an abounding assurance. I completed the poem. My composer brother, George Beverly Shea, set the poem to music, making this a song that's been special to everyone in the Shea family. It's a testimony of God's presence in our lives throughout the years, a presence for which we are most thankful.

DEVOTIONAL INTERLUDE

In the Presence of the Lord

HAPPY ARE THOSE WHO HEAR THE JOYFUL CALL TO WORSHIP, FOR THEY WILL WALK IN THE LIGHT OF YOUR PRESENCE, LORD.   PSALM 89:15, NLT

Those who knew Jesus when He lived on this earth had the privilege of experiencing His physical presence. They were able to listen to Him teach and to converse with Him. They could see His miracles: healing blind eyes and paralyzed legs, feeding thousands with one small lunch, walking on water, and stopping a storm.

However, when David said to the Lord that those who joyfully worship "will walk in the light of your presence," he was basing those words simply on God's spiritual presence. Like us, David didn't have an opportunity to experience God's physical presence on earth.

But unlike David, we can look back and read about Jesus' "nail-scarred hands, outstretched in love." Through Scripture, Jesus' life on earth is made real to us. And through the power of the Holy Spirit, we can recognize God's presence with us at this very moment.

Lord, how thankful I am that I can pray, for prayer brings me into Your holy presence. I need not wait till the day when I see You face-to-face. I can be confident right now that You are with me!

bfs

I Will Praise Him

I will praise Him in the morning
When the day is new and bright;
I will praise Him at the noontime
When the sun is at its height.
I will praise Him in the evening
When the sun is sinking low,
And His love will then enfold me,
As in prayer to Him I go.

I will praise Him for the sunshine,
And my blessings ev'ry day;
I will praise Him in the shadow
Of the trials He sends my way,
And when sorrows fill my mornings
I will think of joys to come,
For I know He guides my future,
And I'll praise His plan well done.

I will praise Him in the morning,
In the evening,
All the time.

Words and Music: George Beverly Shea (b. 1909)
Words, stanza 2: Elaine Shea Anderson (b. 1950)
Copyright © 1972 by Word Music Inc. All rights reserved. Used by permission.

*T*his simple little song came to me some years ago while I was living about twenty miles from downtown Chicago in the suburb of Western Springs. One morning I was trying to fix our television set. Not knowing much about electronics, I soon became frustrated. Looking out the window, I saw how brightly the sun was shining—what a beautiful morning it was!

I knew that we are to praise the Lord in every circumstance. Going to the piano and playing a loud chord in the key of C, I repeated it many times and struck a few loud bass notes for good measure! Then the sunshine inspired me to start singing, "I will praise Him in the morning when the day is new and bright." I completed this verse and chorus and left it for a few days, not realizing that it would almost become a theme song to warm up the vocal cords on many occasions.

When my daughter, Elaine, came to visit a few days later, I sang her the new song. She listened and said, "But, Dad, it's too short."

"Why don't you write a second verse?" I asked. Within five minutes, she had written the second stanza, which I like to call the better of the two.

A few weeks later while traveling with Cliff Barrows, we somehow became separated at London's Heathrow airport. As I looked for him, I heard echoing along the hallways the sound of someone whistling, "I Will Praise Him." I had found Cliff!

Those words minister to each of us, because we all go

through difficult times. I'm thankful for the second verse, words of encouragement that God gave to our dear Elaine, thoughts to remind us that God does not forsake those who love Him.

In 1997, I was privileged to have my daughter sing this with me on the program *George Beverly Shea and Friends*. George Hamilton IV was the master of ceremonies for this special evening. The program was produced by Donna and Susan Campbell for University of North Carolina Television and broadcast on PBS.

DEVOTIONAL INTERLUDE

Praising God All the Time

I WILL SING UNTO THE LORD AS LONG AS I LIVE: I WILL SING PRAISE TO MY GOD WHILE I HAVE MY BEING.   PSALM 104:33, KJV

IN EVERY THING GIVE THANKS: FOR THIS IS THE WILL OF GOD IN CHRIST JESUS CONCERNING YOU.

1 THESSALONIANS 5:18, KJV

"Everything that lives" is commanded to praise the Lord (Psalm 150:6, NLT). There are many reasons for praising God. He is powerful, faithful, loving, merciful, and forgiving. He has brought us salvation and will never leave us. He gives us His strength when we face trials and sorrows. The lists of His characteristics and His gifts are unending.

Even when our circumstances are less than perfect, we can express our thankfulness to God for being with us in each and every situation. No matter what we go through, we can please Him with our praises all day.

Dear Lord, I praise You for each new morning, for the strength You give me every day, and for the love with which You surround me at the end of the day. I praise You for blessings and for staying with me through trials and sorrows. May I continually proclaim the glory of Your name.

bfs

The Wonder of It All

There's the wonder of sunset at evening,
The wonder of sunrise I see;
But the wonder of wonders that thrills my soul
Is the wonder that God loves me.

O the wonder of it all!
The wonder of it all!
Just to think that God loves me.
O the wonder of it all!
The wonder of it all!
Just to think that God loves me.

There's the wonder of springtime and harvest,
The sky, the stars, the sun;
But the wonder of wonders that thrills my soul
Is a wonder that's only begun.

Words and Music: George Beverly Shea (b. 1909)

So many of us have had the experience of traveling long hours on a highway, alone at the wheel on an all-day journey, often extending into the shadows of night. Perhaps like me you are remembering that the distances did not seem as tedious when the person to whom you were wedded was a precious companion by your side. You would talk about the beautiful scenery or chuckle at some unusual sight. My precious companion's name was our Erma. We were together on "that road" for forty-two years.

I recall one of the more lonely times. When the radio was fading into the distance, I turned the dial and a voice I recognized as my own was ringing out above the sound of the roaring engine of a passing eighteen-wheeler:

> *O the wonder of it all!*
> *The wonder of it all!*
> *Just to think that God loves me.*

Before that recording session in Nashville long ago, I asked the Lord to bring spiritual uplift to the listener. Little did I know that the echo of our song would reach into my own heart in a special way in the distant future.

"The Wonder of It All" was written in the middle of the night on a ship bound for England in 1955. We were on the SS *United States*—the fastest passenger liner on the seas, they told us. Walking in the evening on deck with my six-year-old son, Ron, I met a gentleman I recognized as the president of a New York publishing company. I was

surprised and delighted when my son extended his hand
to the tall man and said, "Pleased to meet you, sir." We
began talking. Soon we stepped inside, out of the chilling
breeze, and dropped into deeply upholstered chairs in the
salon.

I noted that our new friend was of another faith. He
shared his love of great classical music but also spoke of his
enjoyment of the hymns of the church. Soon we were talking about the upcoming Glasgow crusade. He wanted to
know why so many attended such meetings, filling the
great stadiums of the world. "What goes on?" he asked. I
mentioned the necessary weeks of preparation for each event
and the beautiful volunteer choir led by Cliff Barrows. Then
I began to speak of the message of God's love extended to
everyone, and so eloquently expressed by the gracious southern gentleman, Billy Graham. Quoting John 3:16—"For
God so loved the world that He gave His only begotten
Son, that whoever believes in Him should not perish but
have everlasting life" (NKJV)—I found myself quickly
adding, "Oh, sir, if you could see it, the wonder
of it all!"

Perhaps because our new friend was a music publisher,
he reached into his pocket, pulled out an envelope, and
wrote something in large letters. He flashed in front of me
these words: "The Wonder of It All." He said, "I challenge
you to write a song with this title." I smiled, saying that
I had only written a few songs in my life, but thanked him
warmly.

But, you know, there had been a marvelous sunset over
the ocean in the evening. About two o'clock in the morning
Erma whispered, "What are you doing?" "Oh, just working
on a little music," I told her. She knew.

In the morning the ship was rolling a little, but I made it to the desk where we found the rough draft, words and music, to the new song.

There's the wonder of sunset at evening,
The wonder of sunrise I see.
But the wonder of wonders that thrills my soul
Is the wonder that God loves me.

Oh, dear friend reading these words, it *is* "a wonder that's only begun!"

The Wonder of All Things

THOSE WHO LIVE AT THE ENDS OF THE EARTH STAND IN AWE OF YOUR WONDERS. FROM WHERE THE SUN RISES TO WHERE IT SETS, YOU INSPIRE SHOUTS OF JOY.   PSALM 65:8, NLT

LONG AGO THE LORD SAID TO ISRAEL: "I HAVE LOVED YOU, MY PEOPLE, WITH AN EVERLASTING LOVE."   JEREMIAH 31:3, NLT

What a wonderful God we worship! He not only created the sun, moon, and stars, but He gave us sunrises and sunsets. Then there is the most wonderful gift of all—His love!

God loves us so much that He gave His only Son so that we might "have eternal life" (John 3:16, NIV). What a wonder it is that God draws His creation to Himself!

1 Corinthians 13 describes a perfect love, which we try to express but often fail to do. God, who *is* love, however, never fails to show His love to us.

> *O Lord, You are the Creator of all things; and yet, wonder of wonders, You love me. Your love is patient and kind, Lord. It never gives up on me. How I thank You for Your wonderful gift of pure, holy love. Please fill my heart with expectant wonder as I think about Your love for me.*
>
> bfs

Early in the Morning

Early in the morning while the world is still,
Before the daylight streaks the sky,
I would know His will.
I commune with Him, my Savior,
And listen carefully,
And gain the strength I need from Him
While praying quietly.

Thank you, Lord, for hearing me,
Thank you, Lord, for knowing who I am.
Thank you, Lord, for seeing me.
It's so easy to get lost these days
In the shuffle and the noise.

Why not try to do this
When you wake up in the night,
And problems race into your mind
And sleep becomes a fight?
Try this simple method,
You soon will gain control,
And rest will surely come again,
And a calm come o'er your soul.

When I was with Billy Graham in Korea for a large outdoor meeting, one day he smilingly suggested to me that he and Ruth thought ten years was long enough for me to be a widower. Mr. Graham made reference to Karlene, who had worked in his North Carolina office some fourteen years. I was pleased to hear her name, because I had seen her at a team meeting. I asked if she would be at the one in Mesa, Arizona. Mr. Graham said, "Oh, yes, she'll be there."

Well, the Mesa meeting came, and I called Karlene to ask if she would have breakfast with me in the hotel restaurant. I didn't plan what happened as we arrived at the table, but I heard myself saying, "The last time I talked on the phone to your pastor (the Rev. Dr. Calvin Thielman), he asked me, 'When are you coming down here to marry Karlene?'" The utterance surprised me, and I thought to myself, *Did I just say that out loud?* She laughed, then I laughed—this, our first conversation!

In a later letter to Karlene I wrote, "I may be the only team member who has not seen the Biltmore house." I asked if she would join me in a visit to that famous landmark in nearby Asheville. Before long I was extending my trips to include North Carolina.

Not long after, I attended a birthday celebration along with Ruth Graham. She was carrying what I thought was a small parcel of gifts. She asked me to place it by my chair. When everyone was happily conversing, I was surprised to see Ruth motioning for me to open the parcel.

I discovered little pieces of kindling and a box of

matches. In Ruth's attractive backhand, she had written, "Bev, when the farmer's mule stalls, what does he do? He lights a fire under him!"

It was, of course, all in fun. Ruth is so well known for her creativity and thoughtful, encouraging words—just one of the reasons everyone loves her so much.

Soon after that evening, Karlene heard my recording of Kurt Kaiser's song "Early in the Morning" on the radio. She heard this:

"Thank you, Lord, for hearing me,
Thank you, Lord, for knowing who I am.
Thank you, Lord, for seeing me.
It's so easy to get lost these days
In the shuffle and the noise."

Karlene prayed, "You know me, Lord, and I place it all in Your hands."

And so it was. Christmas was near, and we were married in the Graham home. As the Christmas lights twinkled on the tree, the Reverend Dr. Calvin Thielman donned his Sunday morning robe and read the vows. Karlene and I were married in a candlelight ceremony, standing by the fireplace, which was decorated with garland. Engraved inside the ring Karlene gave to me were these words: "The Wonder of It All" Psalm 28:7 (the reference of the verse I've signed so many times).

Our wonderful adventure began in December, 1985. Yes, her name is my beloved Karlene.

And the adventure continues. We are thanking the Lord, continually surprised and delighted by the opportunity of serving Him together in so many places. Little did we know that this event would take us to San Francisco, Vancouver, London, Hong Kong, and way beyond.

DEVOTIONAL INTERLUDE

My Savior Knows Who I Am

O LORD, YOU HAVE EXAMINED MY HEART AND KNOW
EVERYTHING ABOUT ME. YOU KNOW WHEN I SIT DOWN OR
STAND UP. YOU KNOW MY EVERY THOUGHT WHEN FAR AWAY.
YOU CHART THE PATH AHEAD OF ME AND TELL ME WHERE TO
STOP AND REST. EVERY MOMENT YOU KNOW WHERE I AM.

PSALM 139:1-3, NLT

Early morning is a wonderful time to talk quietly with our
Savior. David knew that when he said, "In the morning I lay
my requests before you" (Psalm 5:3, NIV).

One morning Karlene offered a special prayer to God,
seeking His direction for her life. God was there.

We all face decisions. When we commune regularly with
our Savior and quietly listen for His direction, He is always
there.

*Lord, I want Your direction for every decision I make, big
and small. Thank You for allowing me to talk to You.
Thank You for listening, for understanding, and for
giving rest when I leave everything in Your hands.*

bfs

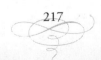

Favorites of Friends

$\mathcal{G}$od uses music to open the heart and the Word
of God to fill it.

—BILL FASIG

Let the Lower Lights Be Burning

Brightly beams our Father's mercy
From His lighthouse evermore,
But to us He gives the keeping
Of the lights along the shore.

Let the lower lights be burning!
Send a gleam across the wave!
Some poor fainting, struggling seaman
You may rescue, you may save.

Dark the night of sin has settled,
Loud and angry billows roar;
Eager eyes are watching, longing,
For the lights along the shore.

Trim your feeble lamp, my brother;
Some poor sailor, tempest-tossed,
Trying now to make the harbor,
In the darkness may be lost.

Words and Music: Philip P. Bliss (1838–1876)

I read that the following story was often told by the great evangelist Dwight L. Moody to help illustrate our responsibility as Christians to direct others to Jesus Christ:

> On a dark, stormy night, when the waves rolled like mountains and not a star was to be seen, a boat, rocking and plunging, neared the Cleveland harbor. "Are you sure this is Cleveland?" asked the captain, seeing only one light from the lighthouse.
> "Quite sure, sir," replied the pilot.
> "Where are the lower lights?"
> "Gone out, sir."
> "Can you make the harbor?"
> "We *must*, or perish, sir!"
> With a strong hand and a brave heart, the old pilot turned the wheel. But alas, in the darkness he missed the channel, and with a crash upon the rocks the boat was shivered, and many a life was lost in a watery grave.

"Brethren," Mr. Moody would say, "the Master will take care of the great lighthouse. *Let us keep the lower lights burning!*"

Hearing Mr. Moody use this illustration at his meetings, Philip Bliss, the singer, songwriter, and evangelist, wrote a poem around the story and then set it to music.

Brightly beams our Father's mercy
From His lighthouse evermore.

God has given us His Word—the Scripture—with the unfolding story of merciful redemption though Jesus Christ, His Son. It is the Light of God's love for us that stirs the soul to life.

But Philip Bliss's song talks about the need for *us* to keep the "lower lights burning" along the shore. Having accepted Jesus Christ as Lord and Savior, people often feel uncertain about reaching out to those around them. Unfortunately many Christians are so busy with work, family commitments, and day-to-day living that they feel their witness is not important. Have you heard people say, "When I retire or when the children go to college or when . . . ?" God has given us the privilege now of being the "lower lights." We can do this by reaching out to others—friends, family, neighbors, those whom we see at work, and others. We may be the only voice these people hear, above the noise and busyness of life, that leads them to the saving grace of Jesus Christ.

We can be the "lower lights" that God uses to break through the darkness. It is a privilege to show His love to others. Sometimes an understanding smile, a listening heart, or a few caring words can reach out to someone, giving an opportunity for God's love to reach out and open the eyes and heart of someone you know.

I remember many years ago at the Cotton Bowl in Dallas, we distributed a match to everyone in the audience. In the darkness, more than eighty thousand people struck their matches as I struck mine. The glow from each little light made a difference, dispelling the darkness as all of the lights together combined to spread light across the entire Cotton Bowl. Our light is important, and God uses us to bring His light to everyone on earth. May we seek to burn brightly for Him.

DEVOTIONAL INTERLUDE

Being Light in the Darkness

YOU, O LORD, KEEP MY LAMP BURNING; MY GOD TURNS MY DARKNESS INTO LIGHT.   PSALM 18:28, NIV

DON'T HIDE YOUR LIGHT UNDER A BASKET! INSTEAD, PUT IT ON A STAND AND LET IT SHINE FOR ALL.   MATTHEW 5:15, NLT

IF YOU ARE ASKED ABOUT YOUR CHRISTIAN HOPE, ALWAYS BE READY TO EXPLAIN IT.   1 PETER 3:15, NLT

The light of God's mercy beams brightly from His light-house. That light emanates from Him and from His Son, Jesus Christ, the "light of the world" (John 8:12, NLT). But God also gives His followers the privilege of reflecting His light. What an incredible responsibility!

We must remember, though, that God never gives us work without empowering us. He keeps His lamp burning within us as we study His Word and commune with Him. He gives us courage to let our light shine and words to offer hope to those "trying now to make the harbor."

> *Thank You, Lord, for allowing me, as Your child, to reflect Your light. Keep me close to You, the source of my light. May Your lamp within me bring hope to those who are struggling in the darkness.*

bfs

In My Heart There Rings a Melody

I have a song that Jesus gave me,
It was sent from heav'n above;
There never was a sweeter melody,
'Tis a melody of love.

In my heart there rings a melody,
There rings a melody with heaven's harmony;
In my heart there rings a melody,
There rings a melody of love.

I love the Christ who died on Calv'ry,
For He washed my sins away;
He put within my heart a melody,
And I know it's there to stay.

'Twill be my endless theme in glory,
With the angels I will sing;
'Twill be a song with glorious harmony,
When the courts of heaven ring.

Words and Music: Elton M. Roth (1891-1951)

In My Heart There Rings a Melody

TEDD SMITH, PIANIST AND PLATFORM ARRANGER
FOR THE BILLY GRAHAM CRUSADES, WRITES:

*N*ot many people are given a great singing voice, but everyone can have a song. The psalmist explains the source of the music:

> I waited patiently for the Lord; and he inclined unto me, and heard my cry. He brought me up also out of an horrible pit, out of the miry clay, and set my feet upon a rock, and established my goings. And he hath put a new song in my mouth, even praise unto our God; many shall see it, and fear, and shall trust in the Lord. (PSALM 40:1-3, KJV)

This new song that God gives us may have no words whatever, no melody, no rhythm, and no harmony. This is a "song in the heart." The hymn title, "In My Heart There Rings a Melody," is based on the words of the apostle Paul in Ephesians 5:19 (KJV): ". . . singing and making melody in your heart to the Lord."

What is the "song in the heart"? The final refrain of the song describes it as a "melody of love." It comes from God's love for us, as well as from our love for God and other people.

Elton Menno Roth, the hymn's writer, was for many years a distinguished church musician—a singer, composer, and conductor. In the 1930s after serious study with several prominent teachers, he organized professional choirs that achieved national recognition in their concert tours.

Roth once said that this hymn was written while he was conducting an evangelistic meeting in Texas. As he recalls:

One hot summer afternoon I took a little walk to the cotton mill just outside of town. On my way back through the burning streets of this typical plantation village, I became weary with the oppressive heat and paused at a church on the corner. The door being open, I went in. There were no people in the pews, no minister in the pulpit. Everything was quiet, with a lingering sacred presence. I walked up and down the aisle and began singing, "In my heart there rings a melody," then hurried into the pastor's study to find some paper. I drew a staff and sketched the melody, remaining there for an hour or more to finish the song, both words and music.

That evening I introduced it by having over two hundred boys and girls sing it at the open-air meeting; after which the audience joined in the singing. I was thrilled, as it seemed my whole being was transformed into a song.[6]

I suppose there has never been a time in my own life that I have not sung this song at some Christian gathering, or played it as a piano solo arrangement. It has always given me great pleasure through its joyful melodic line, but has also spoken at other levels.

It is a song of joy, not merely happiness or pleasure, but an eternal joy that persists through all the sorrows and tragedies of life. It is a song of peace and serenity that gives poise and maturity amid the pressures of our present-day living, making the Christian faith something that is vital and everlasting.

---

[6]George H. Shorney and Donald P. Hustad, *Dictionary Handbook to Hymns for the Living Church* (Carol Stream, IL: Hope Publishing, 1978).

Devotional Interlude

The Song That Jesus Gave

Make a joyful noise unto the Lord, all ye lands.
Serve the Lord with gladness: come before his presence with singing. . . . Enter into his gates with
thanksgiving, and into his courts with praise: be
thankful unto him and bless his name.

Psalm 100:1-2, 4, KJV

There's a melody that rings in each heart where Jesus lives.
It's a sweet melody—one that speaks to our soul of God's
love.

People everywhere can sing this melody and understand
it when they hear folks from other lands making "a joyful
noise" with it. Someday all who love the Lord Jesus Christ
will sing together with the angels "when the courts of
heaven ring."

In the meantime, what a blessing it is to express our
thankfulness to God for his love, grace, and mercy. Our
words, thoughts, and feelings of gratitude harmonize with
the angels in heaven even now, for we've begun to sing our
melody of love. It's a song that will never end.

Lord Jesus, I'm so thankful for the melody You've put in
my heart. No matter what circumstances I must face, the
song will continue forever—praise Your name.

bfs

I Will Sing of My Redeemer

I will sing of my Redeemer
And His wondrous love to me;
On the cruel cross He suffered,
From the curse to set me free.

Sing, O sing of my Redeemer,
With His blood He purchased me;
On the cross He sealed my pardon,
Paid the debt and made me free.

I will tell the wondrous story,
How, my lost estate to save,
In His boundless love and mercy,
He the ransom freely gave.

I will praise my dear Redeemer,
His triumphant power I'll tell,
How the victory He giveth
Over sin and death and hell.

I will sing of my Redeemer
And His heav'nly love to me;
He from death to life hath brought me,
Son of God with Him to be.

Words: Philip P. Bliss (1838–1876)
Music: James McGranahan (1840–1907)

I Will Sing of My Redeemer

CLIFF BARROWS, CHOIR DIRECTOR AND PLATFORM EMCEE FOR THE
BILLY GRAHAM CRUSADES, WRITES:

For the last hundred years, "I Will Sing of My Redeemer" has been a rich part of our musical heritage, often sung in churches around the world.

How this wonderful hymn was preserved to become a part of church hymnody is in itself a fascinating account.

Philip Bliss was born on July 9, 1838, in a log cabin in Clearfield County, Pennsylvania. The story is told that Philip soon developed an interest in music. At the age of ten he was thrilled to hear piano music for the first time in his life. Listening for a while, completely entranced, he entered the house from where the music had come and sat enthralled. When the music stopped, the child who hungered for music cried, "Oh, lady, play some more." However her response was to have him escorted from the house!

Philip left home at the age of eleven to work in the lumber camps. In the evening, he attended what was known as a "singing school," conducted by hymn writer William Bradbury. In 1850, at the age of twelve, Bliss made his first public confession of Christ.

In the early nineteenth century, music training in America was largely centered on these "singing schools." Classes were often held in schoolhouses, churches, or town halls and were organized by a person who traveled from community to community.

The schools were often known for their strong spiritual emphasis. Many of America's early gospel musicians started out as "singing school" teachers. For over one hundred years, these schools had a profound impact on the quality of congregational and choir singing in churches across America.

In 1858, Philip Bliss was living and working in Rome, Pennsylvania. He boarded with the family of O. F. Young, and while living in their home he met and fell in love with their daughter Lucy. They were married on June 1, 1859. A year later, he began his career as an itinerant music teacher. During the winter months he traveled from place to place with a small folding organ. Then, during the summer of 1860, Philip was himself a student at the Normal Academy of Music in Genesco, New York.

Bliss met evangelist D. L. Moody in 1869, and the two worked together over the following years. Bliss was fast becoming a great singer of gospel music.

In 1870, Bliss heard a sermon by evangelist Major D.W. Whittle, which inspired him to write, "Hold the Fort, for I Am Coming." Whittle was invited to address a convention and was asked to bring a singer. Mr. Moody was consulted and Bliss was chosen.

In September 1876, Bliss again met with Moody in Chicago, where Moody talked the Blisses into helping out in eleven meetings in one week. There had also been requests for Bliss to visit England, and Moody encouraged him to go. They planned to hold a meeting in Chicago, and then, after the Christmas holidays, go to England. However, it was almost Christmas, and Philip Bliss went back to Rome, Pennsylvania, to spend the holidays with his family.

On December 29, 1876, thirty-eight-year-old Philip P. Bliss was traveling with his wife, returning from the Christ-

mas visit to his family. Near Ashtabula, Ohio, a collapsed
bridge caused the train to plunge onto the icy riverbed
below. Fires broke out from overturned and broken stoves
on the train cars and swept through the wreckage. Surviving
the wreck, Bliss crawled out through a window of the train,
only to return to look for his wife. Reunited, they died
together in the flames.

Bliss's trunk was salvaged from the wreckage, and in it,
among other compositions, was found "I Will Sing of My
Redeemer."

Bliss had a natural ability for both writing lyrics and
composing music. He is credited with writing more than one
hundred hymns. During his short career, Philip Bliss earned
more than thirty thousand dollars (considered a fortune) in
royalties alone. But remembering the poverty of his youth, he
gave all but a modest livelihood to worthy causes.

Set Free by My Redeemer

YOU KNOW THAT GOD PAID A RANSOM TO SAVE YOU FROM THE EMPTY LIFE YOU INHERITED FROM YOUR ANCESTORS. AND THE RANSOM HE PAID WAS NOT MERE GOLD OR SILVER. HE PAID FOR YOU WITH THE PRECIOUS LIFEBLOOD OF CHRIST, THE SINLESS, SPOTLESS LAMB OF GOD.

1 PETER 1:18-19, NLT

Jesus Christ, who has been one with God the Father from the beginning, has such love for us that He was willing to leave heaven to become our Redeemer. He arrived in a world that had been cursed since the Fall, and He stayed until He had paid the price to redeem or ransom us from that curse of sin.

God's offer of freedom from the guilt and punishment of sin is the ultimate gift anyone could ever receive. It's an offer made available to us all through Jesus.

No one but Jesus, the loving and merciful Son of God, could give us victory over sin. No one but He could lead us from "death to life." What a wonderful Redeemer He is!

My Savior and Redeemer, I praise You for the freedom I have in You. Sin and death no longer have a hold on me, because You paid the ransom for my soul at Calvary. May I never stop singing redemption's song.

bfs

I Love to Tell the Story

I love to tell the story of unseen things above,
Of Jesus and His glory, of Jesus and His love;
I love to tell the story because I know 'tis true,
It satisfies my longings as nothing else can do.

I love to tell the story!
'Twill be my theme in glory—
To tell the old, old story
Of Jesus and His love.

I love to tell the story; more wonderful it seems
Than all the golden fancies of all our golden dreams.
I love to tell the story, it did so much for me;
And that is just the reason I tell it now to thee.

I love to tell the story—'tis pleasant to repeat
What seems, each time I tell it, more wonderfully
   sweet;
I love to tell the story, for some have never heard
The message of salvation from God's own
   holy Word.

I love to tell the story, for those who know it best
Seem hungering and thirsting to hear it like the rest;
And when in scenes of glory I sing the new,
   new song,
'Twill be the old, old story that I have loved so long.

Words: Arabella K. Hankey (1834–1911)
Music: William G. Fischer (1835–1912)

DONALD HUSTAD, ORGANIST/EDUCATOR FOR THE
BILLY GRAHAM CRUSADES (1960–1970) WRITES:

*I*n today's "information era," verbal storytelling may well
be considered a pleasant, but largely irrelevant pastime.
However, evangelical scholars agree that all human communication was originally an "oral tradition"—that, for
instance, the first pages of Scripture were originally passed
on from one generation to another in spoken stories. Later,
these were written down with the inspiration of the Holy
Spirit.

Even today in remote primitive cultures that don't have
a written language, storytelling is the only source of history,
of information, and of news. In those communities, certain
individuals achieve recognition and high honor because of
their ability to remember and tell the narrative that gives the
culture its identity and reveals its understanding of the
universe and human existence.

So here is the story of a hymn written by an English
woman in the nineteenth century. Arabella Katherine
Hankey, who lived from 1834 to 1911 and was usually
called Kate, grew up in the home of a Christian banker in
London, England. The family worshiped with an evangelical
sect called the "Clapham group," which was associated with
William Wilberforce, an important statesman and humani-
tarian who is especially remembered for his work to abolish
the slave trade.

Kate never married and spent her entire life in religious
activities: teaching Bible classes for working women,
supporting foreign missions, and visiting the sick. In 1866,

she became seriously ill, and during a long period of convalescence she wrote a poem of fifty stanzas in two parts, based on the life of Christ and called "The Old, Old Story." In the first section, she included stanzas that were later set to music and published as a gospel song entitled "Tell Me the Old, Old Story." In the latter part of the poem, she included other stanzas that begin, "I love to tell the story." None of Miss Hankey's original poem was intended to be sung, but those two songs are still heard in churches today.

"I Love to Tell the Story" explains *why* the singer loves to tell this story: first, "because I know 'tis true;" second, because "it satisfies my longings as nothing else can do"; third, because "some have never heard the message of salvation from God's own Holy Word"; and fourth, because "those who know it best seem hungering and thirsting to hear it like the rest."

Actually, in these lines, Kate Hankey gives only a broad outline of the actual story she loved to tell—and did tell in the remaining, unsung lines of her long poem. The story is not confined to the thirty-three years of Jesus' earthly life. It begins in the glory of God's eternal presence, when God the Father, Son, and Holy Spirit purposed to create the universe, which would contain a planet called Earth. This planet would be the home of a human race with whom God would share His love and His fellowship.

The poem continues with a description of the actual work of creation narrated in Genesis 1 and includes the failure of the first human beings to respond properly to God's loving gifts. The story tells of God's continuing actions to save His people, especially through His covenants with Abraham and Moses, and His mighty, loving deeds on behalf of the Hebrew people.

The narrative reaches its climax when God's eternal Son renounces His glory to live among us humans, to minister to all human need, to show us how we should live and serve Him, and finally, to die on the cross and rise again from the dead to make that possible.

Yet the story goes on. Jesus ascended into heaven, where He now acts as our Intercessor, pleading our cause with the Father. One day He will return to take believers to live eternally in God's presence, where "telling the story" will be our joyful, unending occupation!

Finally, this is not just one story among many. In all the world's libraries, this is *the* story—the most important story in all history. For every human being is included in that story of "Jesus and His love."

Telling the Story

COME AND LISTEN, ALL YOU WHO FEAR GOD, AND I WILL TELL YOU WHAT HE DID FOR ME. PSALM 66:16, NLT

THEN THE TWO FROM EMMAUS TOLD THEIR STORY OF HOW JESUS HAD APPEARED TO THEM AS THEY WERE WALKING ALONG THE ROAD AND HOW THEY HAD RECOGNIZED HIM AS HE WAS BREAKING THE BREAD. LUKE 24:35, NLT

As followers of Christ, we are encouraged to witness to others about our faith. The word *witness* is seldom used in our secular culture, except in a courtroom. However, we all enjoy a good story—which is one of the best forms of witnessing. Sitting around a table, everyone listens as we eagerly share the details of a personal experience.

In Scripture we like to read the stories of what God did for people like Ruth, David, and Esther. We learn about God's love from the stories Jesus told, and we grow in our faith by reading Paul's story. As God works in the lives of His people today, His loving story continues.

Heavenly Father, there is no greater story than that of Your Son and His love. May I never stop reading it, loving it, and telling it.

bfs

Timeless Classics

*M*usic goes a great way toward preparing people to receive the preaching of the Word. . . . people focus their mind and their heart on the statement that's being made in the song. This is why it's so important that the music we do not be a performance as much as a presentation.

—CLIFF BARROWS

How Great Thou Art

O Lord my God! When I in awesome wonder
Consider all the worlds[7] Thy hands have made.
I see the stars, I hear the rolling[8] thunder,
Thy power throughout the universe displayed.

Then sings my soul, my Savior God to Thee:
HOW GREAT THOU ART! HOW GREAT
   THOU ART!
Then sings my soul, my Savior God to Thee:
HOW GREAT THOU ART! HOW GREAT
   THOU ART.

*W*hen through the woods and forest glades I wander
And hear the birds sing sweetly in the trees,
When I look down from lofty mountain grandeur
And hear the brook and feel the gentle breeze.

*A*nd when I think that God, His Son not sparing,
Sent Him to die, I scarce can take it in;
That on the cross, my burden gladly bearing,
He bled and died to take away my sin.

*W*hen Christ shall come with shout of acclamation
And take me home, what joy shall fill my heart!
Then I shall bow in humble adoration
And there proclaim, my God HOW GREAT
   THOU ART!

Words: Carl Boberg (1859–1940)
English translation: Stuart K. Hine (1899–1989)
Music: Swedish Folk Melody
Copyright © 1953 S. K. Hine. Assigned to Manna Music, Inc., 35255 Brooten Rd., Pacific City, OR 97135. Renewed 1981. All rights reserved. Used by permission. (ASCAP)

---

[7]Author's original word is *works*.
[8]Author's original word is *mighty*.

*S*wedish pastor Carl Boberg wrote the words to this beautiful hymn in 1885 or 1886. He found that his heartfelt expression to God could well be wedded to a melody of the day. "How Great Thou Art" almost immediately became a great favorite of the people, finding its way into hearts and hymnbooks in Sweden and in other European countries, including a Russian translation that was precious to believers there.

The talented linguist Stuart K. Hine, a missionary in Russia, became inspired to translate their magnificent version into the English version we all love so much.

One March afternoon in 1954 on London's Oxford Street, I was given a copy of the Russian words and the English translation by Mr. Andrew Gray of Pickering and Inglis, Ltd. Our beloved colleague Cliff Barrows received his copy that same evening. We were in the city with Dr. Graham for the Harringay Arena Crusade.

Cliff and I began to realize that we had been given a wonderful new hymn, so suitable for both choir and solo voice. After the London meetings closed, Cliff Barrows, pianist Tedd Smith, organist John Innes, and I rehearsed the song with the fine volunteer choir at the Toronto Crusade in the Maple Leaf Gardens.

Coming to the words "consider all the *works* Thy hands have made," I just happened to sing out "*worlds* Thy hands have made." And further, coming to the original text of "I hear the *mighty* thunder," with emphasis I found myself singing "the *rolling* thunder." Cliff Barrows, Mr. Graham's masterful choir director, looked over at me with a smile. I think he was saying, "Fine, Bev, fine."

I first recorded the song in 1956 in the RCA studios in California.

Tim Spencer, of Manna Music and formerly of Sons of the Pioneers, entered into an agreement with Stuart Hine to publish the hymn in North America. Concerning the word changes, Mr. Hine graciously consented to what seemed easier to joyously sing. Soon this hymn was appearing in the new hymnals in North America.

In 1957 at New York's Madison Square Garden, people asked to hear "How Great Thou Art" every night for sixteen weeks. I had the privilege of singing this along with the Crusade choir.

One evening, several weeks into the meeting, I returned to Room 3943 at the New Yorker Hotel. Overlooking the Hudson River from the thirty-ninth floor, I saw the *Queen Mary* docked there with all its lights ablaze. It was late at night, so my wife and seven-year-old son, Ronald, were both asleep. I was thinking of that evening's service, and I wondered to myself, *Did I sing "How Great Thou Art" again tonight?* Why would I question such a thing? Was I so tired or had I sung it so many times that I was just reciting the words and not singing them from my heart? I prayed right there and then, asking the Lord to keep me from failing ever again to be aware of the beautiful words I sing. They continue to be precious to me and touch my heart and soul always.

A gospel singer can have many wonderful experiences when God gives him the privilege to sing hymns and songs that have an impact on many lives—even on the singer. One such experience was in 1966. At the request of the U.S.

military, we traveled to Vietnam. It was a tour of nine different bases.

General Westmoreland met us at the Tan Son Nhut Airport in South Vietnam. From there we went by military helicopter to different compounds. It was the week before Christmas. The team consisted of Billy Graham, Cliff Barrows, Tedd Smith, Dan Piatt, and myself. At times we separated so we could visit as many bases as possible.

One afternoon a young colonel took me in his jeep to a compound where I saw a Christmas tree erected, held up by guy wires. Underneath were beautifully wrapped Christmas presents. In the distance, under some trees, were several GIs who had just come off the line and were waiting for haircuts. I heard a voice saying, "Hey, Shea, sing us 'How Great Thou Art.' " At that moment I silently prayed, *O Lord, help me as You have never helped me before to get this song across.* I cupped my hands and sang, "Then sings my soul, my Savior God to Thee, how great Thou art." After completing the song, I heard voices shouting out, "Thank you, thank you!" How wonderful. What a privilege to sing praises to God, standing by a Christmas tree in Vietnam.

The message continues on. In April of 2002 I was asked to sing this hymn on the television show *Good Morning, America*, with Mr. Bill Gaither at the piano. I sang it again that evening, accompanied by Bill and Gloria Gaither's wonderful singers in their memorable *Homecoming Special* at New York's Carnegie Hall. It truly is a timeless hymn.

DEVOTIONAL INTERLUDE

God's Greatness

HOW GREAT IS THE LORD, AND HOW MUCH WE SHOULD
PRAISE HIM.   PSALM 48:1, NLT

The words of this beautiful song convey many aspects of
God's creation for which we can't help but offer our songs
of praise. It seems incomprehensible not to recognize the
sovereign hand of God in all of nature when we see the vast-
ness of God's universe and the intricate details of a delicate
flower or insect.

But this powerful Creator God is also our "Savior God."
Jesus, who has all of God's greatness within Him, was willing to come as our Savior, offering salvation to each of us.
How humbling it is to know that God's perfect, loving Son
died—and now lives—for you and me.

> *"O Lord my God," I praise You for Your majestic*
> *creation. And I thank You for the love You showed on the*
> *cross. Your love is so great, "I scarce can take it in." I will*
> *never tire of singing to You, my Savior God: "How great*
> *Thou art! How great Thou art!"*

bfs

Just As I Am

Just as I am, without one plea,
But that Thy blood was shed for me,
And that Thou bidd'st me come to Thee,
O Lamb of God I come! I come!

Just as I am, and waiting not
To rid my soul of one dark blot,
To Thee whose blood can cleanse each spot,
O Lamb of God, I come! I come!

Just as I am, tho' tossed about
With many a conflict, many a doubt,
Fightings and fears within, without,
O Lamb of God, I come! I come!

Just as I am, poor, wretched, blind,
Sight, riches, healing of the mind,
Yea, all I need, in Thee to find,
O Lamb of God, I come! I come!

Just as I am, Thou wilt receive,
Wilt welcome, pardon, cleanse, relieve;
Because Thy promise I believe,
O Lamb of God, I come! I come!

Words: Charlotte Elliott (1789–1871)
Music: William B. Bradbury (1816–1868)

*W*hen I was eighteen, my dad had a special week of evangelistic meetings with guest speakers at our church in Ottawa. Each night as the invitation was given to come forward for a public commitment to Christ, I could hardly wait to stand with the congregation and sing "Just As I Am." I could sing and comfort my heart, which was so convicted, rather than make that public confession. I was satisfied just to sing and not go forward.

On Friday night of that week, Dad quietly left the platform and came to me. Placing his hand on my shoulder he said, "Tonight could be the night, Son." That *was* the night I made public my commitment to Christ.

Sometimes when we sing the invitation hymn, we allow our emotions to give us temporary relief from the issues that concern us, without making a deep commitment in our soul. Perhaps that is one of the reasons why Mr. Graham, over the years, has chosen to have the song of invitation sung just by the choir at his evangelistic meetings.

Cliff Barrows tells about an experience we had with news reporters in London in 1966. They expressed the opinion that the emotional appeal of the song "Just As I Am" was the factor that caused people to go forward. Cliff says that he and Billy Graham discussed the importance of making it very clear that it's the Spirit of God who gives people a desire to make a public commitment to Christ. For the whole month of meetings in London, there was no organ music and no choir singing at the invitation time. All that could be heard was the shuffling of feet on the floor of the Earl's Court arena. At the end of the month one reporter wrote, "Give us back the song. The silence is killing us!"

Mr. Graham has written about this song and the importance of an invitational hymn. When he came to faith in Christ in 1937, he didn't go forward until two songs had been sung: "Just As I Am" and "Almost Persuaded." When the final verse of the second song had been sung twice, he went forward. He was grateful that the man of God in the pulpit patiently waited for more responses to the invitation.

Billy Graham names two reasons why "Just As I Am" was chosen to be used after his messages: First, the song repeats an affirmative response, "O Lamb of God, I come," thus verbalizing what people are doing as they come forward. And second, the words give a strong biblical basis for responding to the call of Christ.

Telling the story of Charlotte Elliott, who lived in England, Mr. Graham explains how she wrote the words to this hymn. She was an invalid for much of her life and often felt sad and ineffective because everywhere around her people were busy in their service to God. Tempted to doubt the reality of her spiritual life, she began writing down reasons why she could trust in Christ. From that list came this song, which has been so meaningful to many, many people.

The song has meant much to me in recent years. I remember when my wife Karlene and I were on an airplane, going to the Amsterdam 2000 Conference on Evangelism. The plane was just a few hundred feet off the ground when I noticed it was not gaining altitude. The pilot's voice came over the intercom, saying the airplane had lost a motor, but we had three more to take us out to sea to jettison fuel. Then we would be returning to Newark airport. I was holding Karlene's hand and found myself quietly praying, "Just as I am, without one plea/But that Thy blood was shed for me." If this was our time to meet the Savior, that's the song I wanted to be singing. In forty-five minutes, the airplane returned to the airport.

Bill Gaither filmed the Billy Graham Homecoming videos at The Cove, the training center near Asheville, North Carolina. Cliff and I sat together during filming. Toward the end of the taping, the Gaither choir sang "Just As I Am" over and over again for about ten minutes. It was so beautiful.

I looked at Cliff and saw how touched he was by the music. We understood again why we had been singing this song for such a long time. When the video was released, there were film clips from former Billy Graham meetings, dating back to 1947 and continuing to the present. As we heard the singing in the background, we saw people walking across stadiums and fields in many different places of the world, making their commitment to Christ. We wiped tears away as years of memories flashed across the screen. What evidence of the work of God! Jesus is still holding out His hand to people everywhere, saying, "Come unto me, all ye that labour and are heavy laden, and I will give you rest" (Matthew 11:28, KJV).

Walking Forward to Meet the Savior

HAVE MERCY ON ME, O GOD, BECAUSE OF YOUR UNFAILING LOVE. BECAUSE OF YOUR GREAT COMPASSION, BLOT OUT THE STAIN OF MY SINS. WASH ME CLEAN FROM MY GUILT. PURIFY ME FROM MY SIN. PSALM 51:1-2, NLT

BEHOLD! THE LAMB OF GOD WHO TAKES AWAY THE SIN OF THE WORLD! JOHN 1:29, NKJV

GOD SHOWED HIS GREAT LOVE FOR US BY SENDING CHRIST TO DIE FOR US WHILE WE WERE STILL SINNERS. AND SINCE WE HAVE BEEN MADE RIGHT IN GOD'S SIGHT BY THE BLOOD OF CHRIST, HE WILL CERTAINLY SAVE US FROM GOD'S JUDGMENT. ROMANS 5:8-9, NLT

NOW IS THE TIME OF GOD'S FAVOR, NOW IS THE DAY OF SALVATION. 2 CORINTHIANS 6:2, NIV

God the Father loves us, accepts us, and forgives us. He does this not because of anything we have done, but because Jesus, the Son of God, shed His blood for us. Billy Graham explains that we have "no plea"—no claim on God's love or forgiveness—except that Jesus shed His innocent blood to reconcile us to His Father. We should come just as we are because that's how God loves us. We should come because only Christ can cleanse us and make us presentable to God. We should come in faith, even though we don't understand everything about salvation.

In the busyness of life, it's so easy to put aside things of the spirit. Many of us avoid for too long our "walk down" to the grace, mercy, and love that our Savior freely offers.

As we read and reread the words of this beautiful hymn, we realize that the desire of God's heart is for us to come forward to meet Him. Just as we are, we can come to the Lamb and receive His welcome, His pardon, His cleansing from sin, and His gift of total relief from the guilt of our sin.

O Lamb of God, I come to You "just as I am." I know You left heaven so You could come to earth and give Your spotless blood, which takes away all sin, including mine. Thank You for removing not only the sin but the guilt. Thank You for the peace You give.

bts

A New Song

He's with Me

Oh, wonder of wonders,
The worlds cannot equal;
Nothing can compare
When I hear
My Savior say,
"He's with Me!"

Jesus says, "He's with Me!"
Leave him alone.
The world is calling,
And Jesus says,
"He's with Me!"

The folly of sin,
The foolishness of man
Is only redeemed by our Savior's hand.
"I am not worthy,"
We all want to say;
But Jesus reaches out and says,
"He's with Me!"

He's with Me

$\mathcal{S}$ir David McNee, retired Commissioner of Police of the Metropolis (London, U.K.) based at New Scotland Yard, and the Rev. Dr. Don Wilton joined a group accompanying Billy Graham to the Scottish Parliament, where Mr. Graham was to speak. Dr. Wilton noticed that the chair he chose was unusually comfortable and upholstered in red velvet. Shortly after he sat down, a house security officer approached Sir David. Pointing to Dr. Wilton, the officer asked, "Who is he?"

Sir David authoritatively replied, "He's with me!"

The security guard responded, "It's a good thing, because that man is sitting in the Queen's chair!"

As Chief Inspector at Scotland Yard, Sir David was the only one who could have authorized Dr. Wilton's presence, allowing him to remain in that very special chair.

Dr. Wilton quietly explains that when we come before God someday, we won't be alone—Jesus will be there. And He will say to God the Father, "It's all right. He's with *Me*."

. . . Radio days on ABC
from 1945 to 1953

. . . and on Christian radio
WMBI Chicago, including
KRNT in Des Moines, Iowa

Photographer Russ Busby couldn't resist taking a photo of this police bike in Rio de Janeiro, 1975.

A visit to Winchester, Ontario, for the town's dedication ceremony in 2002. From left: Roy Fawcett, Officer Garth Hampson of the Royal Canadian Mounted Police, and Winchester's Mayor Cousineau.

With George Hamilton IV in 1984. We visited the Cleft in the Rock near England's Cheddar Gorge where August Toplady wrote "Rock of Ages" in 1776.

Singing "This Little Light of Mine" with Cliff Barrows and Billy Graham in Dallas, 1987. Mr. Graham performed a solo after the line, "Hide it under a bushel?" when he sang a firm "No!"

With John Innes at the piano at The Cove, the Billy Graham Evangelistic Association training center near Asheville, North Carolina.

A favorite duet with Cliff Barrows, "Jesus Whispers Peace."

(right) More than 1.1 million people (according to the police) attended the final service of the 1973 Seoul, Korea, crusade.

In 2002 with Franklin Graham, chatting with President
George H.W. Bush in Dallas.

A light moment with Billy and Franklin
at the Dallas Mission in 2002.

At the British Embassy
in Washington, D.C.,
2001, with Karlene
for the knighting
of Dr. Billy Graham.

At home with Karlene in North Carolina.

In 2001, the renowned portrait artist, John Howard Sanden,
presented this portrait to Houghton College in New York,
where it remains today in the music library.

Alphabetical Index of Songs

About the Author

Based on material from the Billy Graham Evangelistic Association

Since George Beverly Shea first sang for Billy Graham on the Chicago radio hymn program *Songs in the Night* in 1943, he has carried the gospel in song to every continent and every state in the Union. He is the recipient of ten Grammy nominations, one Grammy Award (1965), and is a member of the Gospel Music Association Hall of Fame (1978).

As the musical mainstay in Mr. Graham's crusades, Bev Shea is often called "America's Beloved Gospel Singer." Born in Winchester, Ontario, February 1, 1909, where his father was a Wesleyan Methodist minister, Mr. Shea's first public singing was in the choir of his father's church. Later, he sang with the Houghton (N.Y.) College Glee Club.

Added to Billy Graham Crusade, radio, and television dates in many countries, Mr. Shea has sung hundreds of concerts and recorded more than seventy albums of sacred music—including nine CDs. Every hymn he sings is a testimony to the saving power of Jesus Christ and to Shea's faith in Him. He is also a noteworthy composer.

Mr. Shea has utilized all available media to share the Good News of Jesus Christ. From 1952 on, he was heard regularly on network radio, and in more recent years his bass-baritone voice has been transmitted on weekly shortwave programs around the world.

Mr. Shea's network radio singing started on *Club Time*, a program carried for more than eight years on ABC, the Armed Forces network, and many independent stations. When Billy Graham, then pastor of the Village Church in Western Springs, Illinois, took over *Songs in the Night* on Chicago's WCFL in 1943, he recalled hearing Shea's radio singing and enlisted him to help with the radio broadcast.

That was the beginning of a long association between Mr.

Graham and Mr. Shea. In 1947 Shea went to Graham's hometown, Charlotte, North Carolina, to sing in the first of Mr. Graham's citywide crusades, now called missions.

The fledgling evangelistic team worked together in several other crusades, and in 1949 the famous Los Angeles tent meetings catapulted Mr. Graham and his associates to national attention. From there, the team went on to share the gospel on every continent.

Because of Mr. Shea's weekly singing on *The Hour of Decision* radio broadcast since 1950 and his numerous personal appearances, his voice is recognized now in Africa, Asia, Australia, Europe, South America, and throughout North America.

Since the beginning of Mr. Graham's ministry, Shea and Cliff Barrows have been the nucleus of the musical team. Barrows is choir director, platform emcee, and radio-television program director. They were joined in 1950 by pianist Tedd Smith, and through the years, organists Don Hustad, John Innes, and Bill Fasig have provided additional accompaniment.

Mr. Shea is noted for the simplicity of his faith and testimony. All his life and work is aimed at telling "of the Christ who died for me."

For his significant contributions to gospel music, he was inducted into the Religious Broadcasting Hall of Fame (NRB) in February 1996. In 1998 the North Carolina Public Broadcasting Station produced Mr. Shea's life story, *The Wonder of It All,* titled after one of his most popular gospel songs.

Mr. Shea and his wife, Karlene, make their home in North Carolina.

Note from the Publisher

BETTY FREE SWANBERG
Senior Editor and Staff Writer, Tyndale House Publishers

What's it like to visit with George Beverly Shea? Try to imagine
the scene outside the car window as he takes you for a drive
through the beautiful Blue Ridge Mountains. Or picture yourself
at a local restaurant, eating and talking and listening as he says
something pleasant and encouraging to each server and busboy.

Then think about what it would be like to sit in his living
room, where he and his wife welcome you to their home with
coffee and cookies. You suddenly realize you're spending the day
with Billy Graham's famous longtime soloist, who is known
around the globe. You're with a humble man who loves people
everywhere—and they love him back.

You enjoy hearing Mr. Shea talk about past experiences with
composers, singers, and others who enjoy music. As he speaks, he
breaks into song, recalling from memory a favorite stanza from a
hymn or gospel song. Or Bev may give you the privilege of listening with him to some of his favorite CDs. The music might
include a classical number, with loud bass notes vibrating through
the home. Or perhaps you hear the haunting, sweet melodies of a
chamber choir from Scotland. Then, of course, you enjoy some
Bev Shea CDs, with everything from foot-stomping country
melodies to majestic hymns, lively spirituals, and melodic gospel
tunes.

Mr. Shea has allowed me to do all of these things as we have
worked together on this book. His associate and friend, Jeff
McKenzie, and I have visited the Sheas several times, interviewing
Mr. Shea. What a joy this has been!

Bev tells me that his connection with Billy Graham has been
a wonderful privilege. And I tell Mr. Shea that I consider it a
wonderful privilege to have had the opportunity of visiting him
and assisting in the writing of this book!

On the following pages are comments from some of his

coworkers and friends. We are including these tributes not to bring glory to Bev Shea, for that is the last thing he would want. We are doing it to show how God ministers through people who are committed to Him.

Notes from the Billy Graham Team of Musicians

CLIFF BARROWS
Music Director, Billy Graham crusades; Radio & TV Program Director

George Beverly Shea has influenced the lives of more Christian artists than any other living musician. His unexcelled gifted artistry, gracious demeanor, humble disposition, love and appreciation for fine gospel songs, hymns, and lyrics have touched the hearts of people around the world.

When traveling to other countries where the Christian message has gone, one hears people inquiring about Bev Shea. They express their appreciation for him and his singing.

One of the songs that Bev Shea sings that has meant the most to me is "How Great Thou Art." He played a major role in introducing this song to North America. Another favorite of mine is "I'd Rather Have Jesus." Bev, of course, wrote the music for that song. My mother gave me a copy of it when I was heading off to college many years ago. She told me to memorize it and sing it whenever I could . . . and added, "Maybe someday you'll have an opportunity to meet Mr. Shea." I never dreamed that five years later that opportunity would be mine! Now I've had over half a century of wonderful fellowship and ministry around the world with him and Mr. Graham.

I believe that since the time of Creation when the morning stars sang together, music has been part of God's grand design. Music provides a way for God to draw us to Himself as we glorify and praise Him in worship. The Spirit of God can use the melodies of our songs, as well as the words, to make an impact upon the hearts of the hearers.

Martin Luther was so convinced of the power of music that he employed it regularly in proclaiming the truth and teaching God's Word. He said, "Next to the Word of God, music deserves the highest praise."

Music can prepare people in an unusual way for the preaching of God's Word. This has been so true in the life and ministry of Bev Shea. He has had the unique privilege of singing the wondrous story just prior to Mr. Graham's telling of that story at the crusades, and he has been greatly used of God in preparing hearts for the Word of God.

When I think of my friend Bev, I think of Stuart Hamblen's song "Until Then," which Bev often sings just before Mr. Graham brings the message. Stuart had a unique ability, through gifted lyrics, to relate spiritual truths to everyday living. I know that as long as Bev lives in "this troubled world," he will "pause to remember" God's goodness to him—and his songs will continue to encourage us to do the same. Even now, in his nineties, we know that his "heart will go on singing . . . until the day God calls [him] home."

BILL FASIG
Team Organist and Pianist

When I began working with the Billy Graham team in 1968, I learned a vital lesson from Cliff Barrows: In the many crusades Mr. Graham has conducted, God uses music to open the heart and the Word of God to fill it. This fact is constantly revealed through the vocal ministry of my friend and colleague Bev Shea. Simplicity of style and integrity of life combine to create the formula of an artist and servant who honors God.

It was Christmas morning of 1941, scant days after Pearl Harbor. At age eleven I was deeply involved in music, having started piano lessons at age seven. In breathless excitement my two older sisters and I were finally allowed to enter the living room. This was Christmas!

Near the Christmas tree stood a large box too big to wrap, which was draped with a dining room tablecloth. "Dad, what is it? Let me see!" I called out.

My father's response was simple: "Everyone close your eyes and open your ears."

With eyes screwed tightly shut, I waited. In a moment I heard the voice of George Beverly Shea singing "I'd Rather Have

Jesus." On the other side of the 78 rpm record was the song "God Understands."

Father had purchased a combination radio/phonograph player as a family Christmas gift. I don't know how many times we played that record and listened to Mr. Shea on radio station WMBI, where he was at that time a staff musician and announcer. Never did the thought occur to me in my young heart that just a few years later I would have the opportunity and challenge to accompany him on organ and piano.

His repertoire of gospel songs was so vast that quite often only the Lord knew what he was about to sing, whether in concert or at a Billy Graham evangelistic crusade. Sometimes at the last second, while walking to the podium, Bev would flash with one hand the key signature of the song he was about to sing. Fingers pointed down indicated the number of flats; pointed up was the number of sharps. For example, three down meant E-flat, while two up meant the key of D. Thus, whoever played the introduction to his song didn't have a clue as to the title of the song. The accompanist's job was simply to get Bev into the right key, then wait for his first words that would identify the song.

Scary? Absolutely! But pure Bev Shea. Through the years I have learned to love and trust this man who has sung the gospel around the world, and at this moment it is my desire to pay tribute to him.*

Don Hustad
Team Organist, 1960–1970

When I graduated from college with a degree in music, I had no idea how I would invest my life and training. I didn't know that a man named George Beverly Shea would significantly affect my future participation in the ministry of Christian music.

On the advice of a friend, I auditioned at WMBI, the radio voice of Moody Bible Institute in Chicago. There, in Studio D, I met and played for a handsome, genial member of WMBI's staff who introduced himself as Bev Shea.

*Editor's note: Shortly after the Dallas 2002 crusade (mission) and the writing of this note, Bill Fasig went to be with the Lord.

Shortly thereafter I began playing organ accompaniments for Bev on the Institute's radio program *Hymns from the Chapel.* Later we worked together for eight years on *Club Time,* a national radio broadcast of hymns sponsored by the Club Aluminum Products Company; Bev was soloist, and I arranged and conducted the music for the small accompanying choir.

Eventually it was my privilege to join Bev for several years on the musical team of the Billy Graham crusades. There, almost always, Bev's solo came just before Billy's strong preaching of the gospel.

John Innes
Team Organist

I first met Bev at a recording session for some broadcasts that were to air during the Billy Graham Chicago Crusade of 1962. At the time I was a junior at Wheaton College. The nervousness I felt was soon dissipated by Bev's warm and friendly manner.

After graduation, my wife and I made our home in Wheaton and subsequently visited quite frequently with Bev and Erma at their home in Western Springs. We often spent our time there singing, as well as playing the piano and Hammond organ in his living room. Bev even served as a baby-sitter for our two older children when we had to leave town for a trip in 1969.

It has been an honor to serve as Bev's accompanist in the Billy Graham crusades since 1967. I regret that I have occasionally put him in the wrong key by missing one of his famous hand signals. However, he has always been understanding and forgiving, for which I'm thankful. I have always considered it to be one of the great privileges of my life to have had a small part in Bev Shea's worldwide ministry.

Tedd Smith
Team Pianist

George Beverly Shea is a gentle man. His singing has always been as natural as speech. He has a large repertoire of favorite hymns and gospel songs that he has sung throughout the years. Bev has always enunciated clearly and distinctly, leaving no doubt as to the Message he seeks to convey.

I have been fortunate in having the privilege of traveling around the world with Bev Shea for most of the Billy Graham crusades. I have also performed in concerts with Mr. Shea in many churches and concert halls. These travels have taken us throughout the United States, Canada, England, Ireland, Scotland, Europe, Scandinavia, Asia, Central and South America, Australia, and New Zealand.

Bev's life has reached me in many ways. I will always be grateful because of the crossing of our paths, both in a personal and a musical way. It has been a special privilege to have had this wonderful ministry with "America's beloved gospel singer."

Notes from Friends in Music

JEFF DEYO
Worship artist, former lead singer and principal songwriter,
SONICFLOOd

Music has always deeply touched and influenced me, and it seems
to spill out from the deep parts of my soul.

I grew up in Denver, Colorado, and went to a traditional
church. We always sang hymns in our church, and I never ques-
tioned or disliked that. But in my high school years I began to
realize that the lyrical and musical language of the songs in church
seemed very distant from the music of everyday life. It was around
this time that I became aware of these simple songs that people
were calling choruses.

At that time I experienced a desire for a more personal relationship with God. Since then I have devoted myself completely to
accomplishing His purpose in my life, which starts with me seeking
His kingdom and His righteousness, and ends with me teaching
and leading people in personal, musical worship to our God.

I seek to balance my worship biblically by including songs,
hymns, and spiritual songs. This has inspired me to take some
"older" songs and make them "new" by reworking the instrumen-
tation.

In the summer of 2000, I went to the last night of the Billy
Graham mission in my hometown of Nashville, Tennessee.
George Beverly Shea sang "I'd Rather Have Jesus," a song I had
sung in my church many times as I was growing up. For some
reason, this song really impacted me that night. I felt that God
was impressing on me that the lyrics and melody of this song
could actually transcend time! Very few songs are like this.

I realized that these words were still the heartbeat of a generation of young people who have been saturated with technology—
the microwave generation. The cry of their hearts is still "I'd
rather have Jesus than anything"—more than fame, money,
success, or power!

I started trying to figure out a way to "translate" this special song for a generation that might mistakenly tune it out because of its more traditional arrangement. I worked with my band, and we came up with the arrangement that is now on my newest worship CD.

I believe this song is serving as a bridge for many to renew their passion and commitment to the Lord. The new arrangement allows for a fresh connection between the worshiper, the melody, and the message.

Here are examples from several of the many e-mails we have received: *We introduced your version of "I'd Rather Have Jesus" a couple of weeks ago, and a number of our seniors commented on how much they enjoyed the old hymn with the new style. . . . "I'd rather have Jesus" is now my heart's cry. That is an awesome song. . . . I have been going through a really tough time involving my church and family, but I know that God is always there. I love the song "I'd Rather Have Jesus" . . . and think it's cool you said that it should be the heart cry of our generation. God is truly seeking people who would rather have Jesus.*

George Beverly Shea's music has personally affected my life, as well as the lives of millions of people around the world. Because of God's grace over his songs, they will continue to transcend time and space, inspiring and discipling the next generation of worshipers!

BILL GAITHER
Inspirational singer, composer, producer

In 1970, just after Gloria and I had written "There's Just Something about That Name," we had the privilege of meeting George Beverly Shea for the first time at his home in the Chicago area. It wasn't long before we were sitting at his piano, so I asked if I could play a song for him. He said yes, and I began to play our simple little chorus, *Jesus . . . Jesus . . . Jesus.* I will always remember how gracious Bev was. He later recorded the song, but the memory of those first moments around his piano has always held particular significance for me.

Thirty years later, while recording a video to honor the

impact of the Billy Graham crusades, we gathered at the Billy Graham Training Center in North Carolina, in the area where Bev had relocated years earlier. Once again he invited us into his home to sit around that same piano. I asked him the same question: "May I play a song for you?" Once again he said yes, and I started playing, *Jesus . . . Jesus . . . Jesus.* He remembered.

What continues to overwhelm me about George Beverly Shea is how this world-class talent remains as gracious today as he was three decades ago.

STEVE GREEN
Inspirational vocalist

I owe to George Beverly Shea much of my appreciation for the hymns.

As the child of missionary parents in Argentina, the only exposure I had to music from back home came to me on our one reel-to-reel recording of Mr. Shea and from the programs we picked up on a shortwave radio. One of our weekly favorites was *The Hour of Decision.* I still remember the rich baritone voice singing the gospel just before Mr. Graham spoke.

Today the hymns are part of my devotional life, study time, and worship leading. While I'm glad for the new expressions of praise, the hymns continue to inspire, instruct, and give the church a vehicle to express adoration.

KURT KAISER
Composer, arranger, concert accompanist

Music ministers to so many because we all respond to a melody in a different way. Last year I listened to a compact disc by the Washington Saxophone Quartet. They play incredibly well, and one of the selections, because of its beauty, brought me to tears. Because the music reached me so deeply, I wept like a child. Add to that lovely melody an equally beautiful text, and the effect is often overpowering.

I never know when a familiar hymn will touch a person's heart. Recently at my church we sang "Blessed Assurance," a hymn that I have heard and played countless times. However, there was something about the melody and text and the fact that it was sung thoughtfully, instead of boisterously, that "grabbed" my young pastor so that he wept throughout its singing.

The music of George Beverly Shea touches people. Why do people respond to Bev's singing? They respond because of the richness of his voice, coupled with a sincerity that speaks straight to the heart.

For over thirty years I have been honored to accompany Bev. We have shared platforms in hundreds of cities across this country and in Canada. Basically, Bev sings three selections, and I play three. We alternate so that Bev does not have to stand for interminable periods of time. I have enjoyed very much doing these concerts in cities and towns where people would not ordinarily hear Bev Shea—places in small-town U.S.A. People love hearing the vignettes that seem to be part of the overflow of Bev's life experiences—so many stories: stories that are poignant, funny, serious, and about wartime.

Bev is not easy to accompany, because he stylizes music in such an individual fashion. As his accompanist, I decided there was no way he would "get away" from me musically, though!

To this day Bev possesses rich overtones in his voice that make all the rest of us sound like children with unchanged voices!

Michael W. Smith
Singer and songwriter

When I was growing up in Kenova, West Virginia, music was always very important in our home. I remember going to church with my family and singing the timeless hymns. Even at that young age I was impacted by these hymns; reading and singing the words was like giving voice to a sermon because the truths in these hymns tell of God's simple message of salvation.

Even as a child, I can remember listening to the deep voice of George Beverly Shea singing as we watched the Billy Graham crusades on television. What an impact the music had—his rich and powerful voice, backed by the choir, brought the words of these hymns to life! Little did I know that I would someday meet this wonderful man.

I first had the opportunity to meet with Mr. Shea at one of Billy Graham's crusades and then again in his home. I was amazed at how casual and easygoing he was. Sitting together, we discussed his favorite topic: music. It was an education for me as Mr. Shea spoke lovingly and passionately about the hymns, sharing how some of them came to be written and how they had touched people's lives. For me this was a great time of learning anew just how much music, particularly the songs of our faith, can so dramatically impact lives. In concerts today I carry those same thoughts with me. We never know who is listening and who will find special strength, hope, or courage as they listen to the music. It is a wonderful privilege.

I consider George Beverly Shea both a friend and a mentor. We have had the opportunity to get together many times since that first meeting. I continue to be inspired by this man who has spent his life bringing the gospel message in song to so many people around the world. Thank you, George Beverly Shea, for your encouragement and friendship.

MICHAEL TAIT
Contemporary vocalist with dc Talk

When I was a little kid growing up in Washington, D. C., I remember watching the Billy Graham hour on TV. I remember listening to Dr. Graham speak. My dad was a pastor, so I would think about my dad as I listened to Dr. Graham. My dad's church was a lot smaller than the stadiums Billy Graham spoke in, but even as a little boy, I knew the messages of these two men were a lot the same.

When we sat down to watch Billy Graham on TV, it was a family affair. Actually, it was required viewing for the Tait family.

Of course, I'd see George Beverly Shea stand up and sing. At that time, I already knew I wanted to be a singer, and I remember wondering to myself how it felt to sing in front of all those people. I could never have imagined that one day I would actually be doing that numerous times with Dr. Graham.

George Beverly Shea's voice was powerful, just as it still is today—very big, loud, and deep. He had such a presence about himself. He stood there and commanded attention—not for himself, but for the God who gave him the gift of music. For many years he has inspired me, and I know he inspired my dad. Now it's cool to actually know Mr. Shea, seeing him whenever dc Talk sings at a Billy Graham evangelistic meeting. He's still "the man" when he's up there delivering messages from God through those beautiful deep notes.

A few years back we were able to record together the song "Because He Lives." That was an awesome experience. Here he is, this eighty-something white guy; and here I am, this twenty-something black guy. Generations apart from each other, we came together on tape to sing this beautiful song that Bill and Gloria Gaither wrote.

When I was a kid, I would never have dreamed in a million years that I would get to sing with George Beverly Shea. But now we will share the memory of that experience forever—even after we get to heaven!

More Friends

A WOMAN DROVE TO VISIT her mother and had to return home alone, knowing she would never see her mother alive again. She told Mr. Shea that she played one of his tapes as she drove and that she continued to listen to it until she arrived home. The music helped her survive the long drive and the time of mourning that followed after her mother went home to the Lord.

GINO MONACO FROM MILAN, Italy, had a studio on Michigan Avenue in Chicago, Illinois. He became Bev's vocal instructor when Bev moved to Chicago from New York. For several years a wonderful Christian woman from Wheaton was the talented pianist for Gino's best students. She often talked to Mr. Monaco about the Lord and continued doing that for a long time. At one point she felt that Gino was not receptive to her witness of the gospel message, so she felt constrained to be quiet for a while; but she continued praying for him. Finally Gino Monaco came to faith in the Lord Jesus through the obedient witness and leading of this fine Christian woman.

When Gino became ill, Bev Shea visited him in the hospital. He brought his former coach a special devotional book that he thought might encourage his friend to seek the Lord. Gino looked at the book and smiled. He said, "Beverly, thank you. Did you know I have become a Christian and I love the Lord?" The faithful witness of a pianist along with earnest prayer brought Gino Monaco into the kingdom of God.

"ALIENATION OF AFFECTION" is when one parent seeks to alienate the children from the other parent. A man sought to do just that, taking his children away from their mother. The mother, a Christian, was understandably devastated and found immeasurable comfort during this time of heart grief by listening to Bev's music. Now, through her life's work, she is very effectively counseling children.

A PROFESSIONAL THERAPIST at a retirement home has reported that patients who have Alzheimer's become calm when they listen to Bev Shea's music.

THE SHEAS ATTENDED A CHURCH SERVICE outside of Milwaukee, Wisconsin, shortly after they were married. Karlene sat in the balcony to enjoy the service. A lady sitting next to Karlene watched Cliff Barrows come up on the platform and said, "Oh, isn't Cliff Barrows a wonderful person?" Smiling, Karlene quietly agreed. Then Cliff introduced Bev, who came up to sing. The little lady grabbed Karlene's arm and said, "I just *love* Bev Shea." Karlene turned, took hold of the lady's arm, and said, "Oh-h-h, I do too!"

Later in the program Cliff came back to the podium and said, "I want you to know that Bev Shea was married recently. His wife is here tonight. Karlene, where are you? Would you stand up, please?"

IN THE SUMMER OF 2002, the town of Winchester, Ontario (Canada), honored Bev by inviting him to unveil their new signs. These signs appear at all five entrances to Winchester, a little town south of Ottawa. The signs read: "The Birthplace of George Beverly Shea."

According to *The Winchester Press,* a crowd of four thousand people filled the Winchester Arena to capacity to hear the voice of Winchester's own native son. This all came about through the efforts of Roy and Shirley Fawcett and the officials of Dundas County.

Bev Shea commented on the privilege of hearing the beautiful tenor voice of the master of ceremonies, Garth Hampson. Mr. Hampson also directed the combined four-hundred-voice choir and joined Mr. Shea and other singers and musicians in an afternoon tribute to the beloved gospel hymns.

Mr. Hampson, a member of the Royal Canadian Mounted Police, recalled the story of how Bev endeavored to become a "Mountie" at the age of eighteen but gave up the idea when he thought he might be posted in the Northern Territories! Mr.

Hampson graciously went on to tell the people that Bev did indeed make it to the Northern Territories and other parts of Canada, as well as around the globe, with his gospel song recordings.

The Ottawa Citizen quoted Bev's accompanist, Sharon Adams, as saying, "It's amazing that he can sing like he does at his age. . . . What's even more important, it gives you such a spiritual uplift just to be around him."

The Winchester Press further quoted Mr. Shea as saying that when people go past the signs with his name on them, they will ask, "Who's that?" But he went on to say that it was so kind of the mayor and the people of Winchester to do this.

SOME YEARS AGO DAN, who was an atheist and feared public speaking, went to a home in North Carolina to repair a fireplace. He had heard that the man living there knew Billy Graham. "So you know Billy Graham, eh?" he said. "Say, you don't mind if I smoke my pipe, do you?" He heard Bev Shea's deep bass voice answer, "Yes, I do know Mr. Graham, and yes, you may smoke."

Dan wrote, "I noticed that the man had one of the kindest faces I had ever seen." He says that Bev "smiled, his eyes were warm and accepting, his demeanor peaceful and humble."

Dan told Bev that he didn't want anything to do with Christianity because so many Christians are hypocrites. Bev suggested that Dan buy a Bible. "Get alone with it and read it for yourself. Then you decide who Jesus is."

Dan followed the advice. Instead of committing suicide, as he had planned to do that week, Dan bought a Bible and came to faith two nights later while reading the book of Acts.

Today Dan is an evangelist in Greece working with OAC (Open Air Campaigners) with his lovely Greek family.

ONE DAY DURING A CANADIAN VACATION, Bev played Dottie Rambo's song "If That Isn't Love" from his album by the same name. He played it very loudly on his boom box, and the words wafted across the yard. A neighbor, with tears in her eyes, asked Bev to replay the song. She wanted to hear the second stanza again, which tells how Jesus remembered a thief who hung beside

Him and "took him to Paradise." These friends later came to the
Ottawa Billy Graham Crusade. Again, God spoke through the
message of a gospel song and led a couple to renewal of faith in
heart and life.

"MANY YEARS AGO A COUPLE began attending First Baptist. The
wife trusted Christ before long; not so the husband. One Lord's
Day morning you [Mr. Shea] were at First Baptist Church as
guest soloist. You had to leave immediately after singing in order
to keep to your recording schedule the next day.

"After the service I saw the husband waiting to talk to me. He
said, 'Pastor, for months I have been able to get by your preaching.
But this morning I couldn't get past Mr. Shea's songs. While he
was singing, I trusted Christ. I would like to make a public profession of faith.' The man was in his seventies. The song you sang was
'If That Isn't Love.'"—*Curt*

IN A LETTER TO MR. SHEA, this woman who knew Bev Shea's
parents writes: "We as a family have treasured your singing for
years. My mother met a Christian family at the church near
Ottawa where your father was pastor, and the family adopted her.
She trained to be a nurse and later came to the United States,
where she met and married my father. Together they established a
Christian home and had two children, my brother and myself.

"My brother graduated from a Bible college and has been
very active at his church as well as in a rescue mission and jail
ministry. His children are all active in local churches, and ten of
his eleven grandchildren have already accepted Jesus Christ as
Savior.

"I served twenty-four years as a missionary nurse with Africa
Inland Mission in Kenya and Sudan.

"Our family is very grateful for the way you and your family
have impacted the lives of four generations in our family!"—*Sally*

"TO SAY THAT WE APPRECIATE your hospitality and generosity
(we love the tapes) would be an understatement. We will surely
cherish our visit for the rest of our lives and will always remember
the expressions on the children's faces when your precious music

echoed through the living room. We continue to pray God's blessings upon your ministry, your lives, and your health."—*Dan, Cindi, and children, a family that visited the Sheas at their home in North Carolina*

"MY PARENTS MET while at St. Paul (now Crown) Bible College. Their first date was to one of your concerts in Minneapolis. Because those were penny-pinching days, the concert was a rare treat for them. They both loved the music so much, and the focus on the goodness of the Lord encouraged their discussion about the things most important to them. That discussion unearthed a common passion for sharing the gospel and helped to further their beginning romance! They haven't had an opportunity to attend another of your concerts, Mr. Shea, but ever since that time they have enjoyed your tapes."—*Ramona*

"SONGS ARE REMINDERS OF GOD'S LOVE and faithfulness toward us, and they are also a lovely reminder of the gift of song you have shared with so many in the world. Your voice is a reminder of what is right in this world."

"THANK YOU FOR YOUR DEDICATION and passion to touch lives with the gospel through music when at times nothing else can."—*Anonymous*

POEM BY RALPH CARMICHAEL
I would like to say how much I enjoyed working with Bev, and in a few lines of verse I'd like to sum up what I see in his life and ministry. I call the poem:

The Gospel Singer

And do you ever wonder
Why God would pick one man
And give him one assignment
To do like no one can,
To sway the hearts of people
In tones so bold and strong,
Yet tender like a sonnet—

A gentle, whispered song—
Then bless him with approval
As others he doth bless,
While countless hearts are opened,
The Savior to confess.
It takes one humble servant
Whose purpose is but one:
"Don't magnify my talent,
Just glorify Thy Son."

Sincerely,
Ralph Carmichael
(From the 1968 RCA recording "Be Still My Soul" by George Beverly Shea).

STEPS TO PEACE WITH GOD

1. GOD'S PURPOSE: PEACE AND LIFE

God loves you and wants you to experience peace and life—abundant and eternal.

THE BIBLE SAYS ...

"We have peace with God through our Lord Jesus Christ." *Romans 5:1, NIV*

"For God so loved the world that He gave His only begotten Son, that whoever believes in Him should not perish but have everlasting life." *John 3:16, NKJV*

"I have come that they may have life, and that they may have it more abundantly." *John 10:10, NKJV*

Since God planned for us to have peace and the abundant life right now, why are most people not having this experience?

2. OUR PROBLEM: SEPARATION

God created us in His own image to have an abundant life. He did not make us as robots to automatically love and obey Him, but gave us a will and a freedom of choice.

We chose to disobey God and go our own willful way. We still make this choice today. This results in separation from God.

THE BIBLE SAYS ...

"For all have sinned and fall short of the glory of God." *Romans 3:23, NIV*

"For the wages of sin is death, but the gift of God is eternal life in Christ Jesus our Lord." *Romans 6:23, NIV*

Our choice results in separation from God.

People (Sinful)   God (Holy)

OUR ATTEMPTS

Through the ages, individuals have tried in many ways to bridge this gap ... without success ...

THE BIBLE SAYS ...

"There is a way that seems right to a man, but in the end it leads to death."
Proverbs 14:12, NIV

"But your iniquities have separated you from your God; and your sins have hidden His face from you, so that He will not hear."
Isaiah 59:2, NKJV

There is only one remedy for this problem of separation.

3. GOD'S REMEDY: THE CROSS

Jesus Christ is the only answer to this problem. He died on the Cross and rose from the grave, paying the penalty for our sin and bridging the gap between God and people.

THE BIBLE SAYS ...

"For there is one God and one mediator between God and men, the man Christ Jesus." *1 Timothy 2:5, NIV*

"For Christ also suffered once for sins, the just for the unjust, that He might bring us to God." *1 Peter 3:18, NKJV*

"But God demonstrates His own love toward us, in that while we were still sinners, Christ died for us."
Romans 5:8, NKJV

God has provided the only way ... we must make the choice ...

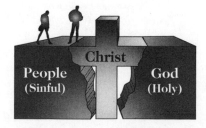

4. OUR RESPONSE: RECEIVE CHRIST

We must trust Jesus Christ and receive Him by personal invitation.

THE BIBLE SAYS ...

"Behold, I stand at the door and knock. If anyone hears My voice and opens the door, I will come in to him and dine with him, and he with Me." *Revelation 3:20, NKJV*

"But as many as received Him, to them He gave the right to become children of God, to those who believe in His name." *John 1:12, NKJV*

"If you confess with your mouth the Lord Jesus and believe in your heart that God has raised Him from the dead, you will be saved." *Romans 10:9, NKJV*

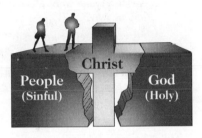

Are you here ... or here?

Is there any good reason why you cannot receive Jesus Christ right now?

HOW TO RECEIVE CHRIST:

1. Admit your need (I am a sinner).
2. Be willing to turn from your sins (repent).
3. Believe that Jesus Christ died for you on the Cross and rose from the grave.
4. Through prayer, invite Jesus Christ to come in and control your life through the Holy Spirit. (Receive Him as Lord and Savior.)

WHAT TO PRAY:

Dear Lord Jesus,

 I know that I am a sinner and need Your forgiveness. I believe that You died for my sins. I want to turn from my sins. I now invite You to come into my heart and life. I want to trust and follow You as Lord and Savior.

 In Jesus' name. Amen.

_____   _____
Date   Signature

GOD'S ASSURANCE: HIS WORD

IF YOU PRAYED THIS PRAYER,

THE BIBLE SAYS ...

"For, 'Everyone who calls on the name of the Lord will be saved.'"
Romans 10:13, NIV

Did you sincerely ask Jesus Christ to come into your life?
Where is He right now? What has He given you?

"For it is by grace you have been saved, through faith—and this not from yourselves, it is the gift of God—not by works, so that no one can boast."
Ephesians 2:8–9, NIV

THE BIBLE SAYS ...

"He who has the Son has life; he who does not have the Son of God does not have life. These things I have written to you who believe in the name of the Son of God, that you may know that you have eternal life, and that you may continue to believe in the name of the Son of God." *1 John 5:12–13, NKJV*

Receiving Christ, we are born into God's family through the supernatural work of the Holy Spirit who indwells every believer. This is called regeneration or the "new birth."

This is just the beginning of a wonderful new life in Christ. To deepen this relationship you should:

1. Read your Bible every day to know Christ better.
2. Talk to God in prayer every day.
3. Tell others about Christ.
4. Worship, fellowship, and serve with other Christians in a church where Christ is preached.
5. As Christ's representative in a needy world, demonstrate your new life by your love and concern for others.

God bless you as you do.

Billy Graham

If you want further help in the decision you have made, write to:
Billy Graham Evangelistic Association,
1 Billy Graham Parkway, Charlotte, North Carolina 28201-0001

A MESSAGE FROM THE BILLY GRAHAM EVANGELISTIC ASSOCIATION

If you are committing your life to Christ, please let us know! We would like to send you Bible study materials to help you grow in your faith.

The Billy Graham Evangelistic Association exists to support and extend the evangelistic calling and ministries of Billy Graham and Franklin Graham by proclaiming the Gospel of the Lord Jesus Christ to all we can by every effective means available to us and by equipping others to do the same.

Our desire is to introduce as many people as we can to the person of Jesus Christ, so that they might experience His love and forgiveness.

Your prayers are the most important way to support us in this ministry. We are grateful for the dedicated prayer support we receive. We are also grateful for those who support us with contributions.

Giving can be a rewarding experience for you and for us at the Billy Graham Evangelistic Association. Your gift gives you the satisfaction of supporting an organization that is actively involved in evangelism. Also, it is encouraging to us because part of our ministry is devoted to helping people like you discover and enjoy the stewardship of giving wisely and effectively.

Billy Graham Evangelistic Association
1 Billy Graham Parkway
Charlotte, North Carolina 28201-0001
www.billygraham.org

Toll-free (U.S.): 1-877-247-2426

Billy Graham Evangelistic Association of Canada
20 Hopewell Way NE
Calgary, Alberta T3J 5H5
www.billygraham.ca

Toll-free (Canada): 1-888-393-0003